Harry,
You are the
Best!

BRAVO —
and thank you.

I DID IT

—Gina Champion-Cain

Also by Neil Senturia

I'm There for You, Baby:
The Entrepreneur's Guide to the Galaxy

I'm Still There for You, Baby:
The Entrepreneur's Guide to the Galaxy

Also by Neil Senturia and Barbara Bry

We're There for You, Baby:
The Entrepreneur's Guide to the Galaxy, Vol. 2

I DID IT

—Gina Champion-Cain

The Largest Woman-Run Ponzi Scheme
in American History

As told to:

Neil Senturia & Barbara Bry

Waterside Productions
Cardiff-by-the-Sea, California

Printed in the United States of America
First Printing, 2022

ISBN-13: 978-1-956503-94-4 (print edition)
ISBN-13: 978-1-956503-95-1 (ebook edition)

Waterside Productions
2055 Oxford Avenue
Cardiff-by-the-Sea, CA 92007
www.waterside.com

"Above all, don't lie to yourself. The man who lies to himself and listens to his own lie comes to a point that he cannot distinguish the truth within him, or around him, and so loses all respect for himself and for others. And having no respect he ceases to love."

—Fyodor Dostoevsky, *The Brothers Karamazov*

Contents

Authors' Note

*Every effort has been made by the coauthors to present a truthful
account of the events described in this book on the basis of the personal
recollections of Gina Champion-Cain; pleadings, depositions,
and other court records; and additional interviews, research, and
reporting. In some instances, conversations are paraphrased based
on the memory of a participant and may not include the actual
words used.*

Prologue

A few facts about Ponzi schemes.

Charles Ponzi is quoted as saying, "I landed in this country with $2.50 in cash and $1 million in hopes, and those hopes never left me."

The first Ponzi scheme was run by two women, Adele Spitzeder and Sarah Howe, in 1869. However, according to the Smithsonian website, in 1906 Ponzi realized that based upon postwar exchange rates, International Reply Coupons purchased in many European nations were worth more in the U.S. than their original cost. He concluded that if he could figure out a way to deal the coupons in a high quantity, he could profit by simply buying and reselling them. Ponzi persuaded a few investors to give him start-up money, promising them a 50 percent profit in 45 days. This was the start of the pyramid scheme that bears Ponzi's name up to the present day.

But it's kind of typical, isn't it, that it was the women who thought it up first, but it was the man who got the credit? What can I tell you? Some things never change.

In the book *The Politics of Ponzi Schemes* by Marie Springer, the author writes: "The qualities we know about Ponzi perpetrators are: they tend to be charismatic, skilled at deception, good at presenting an image of success, glib and knowledgeable, and they make us feel special by participating in the investment."

There have been 3,202 Ponzi schemes over the last 30 years, and women acting alone have only accounted for 120 of them. Now there are 121.

*** ***

CHAPTER 1
The Subpoena
Couldn't they have just called?

May 13, 2019

My name is Gina Champion-Cain. It's a beautiful sunny day in Carmel-by-the Sea, California. I'm sitting on the patio of my vacation home overlooking the Pacific Ocean. I'm excited, yet nervous, about the future. To the outside world, my life looks perfect. After all, I've built a business empire that includes real estate, popular restaurants where it's hard to get a reservation, and trendy retail stores. I'm a guest economics commentator for the *San Diego Union-Tribune*, I serve on prestigious corporate and nonprofit boards, and I'm a role model for young women who want advice on how to succeed in business.

I'm 54 years old, I'm in great shape; and am known for my trade-mark long, jet-black hair; gleaming smile; and very white teeth. I know that men look at me and that I cause a stir when I walk into a room. I've been married for 29 years to Steve Cain, the love of my life. We enjoy golf, biking, and walking our three dogs, and we live in a Craftsman-style home in the Mission Hills neighborhood of San

Diego overlooking the bay. Steve and I don't have children. This was a conscious choice because we've both been focused on our careers, and I did have a hysterectomy several years ago.

And then the phone rings. Joelle Hanson, my executive assistant, calls to tell me that I've received a letter from the Securities and Exchange Commission (SEC). "Should I open it?" she asks.

"No," I say, "just leave it on my desk; it can wait until I'm back in two days."

If it's bad news, I don't want it today, and if it's good news—like, maybe my plan to bundle my businesses together and go public is being reviewed favorably by the investment bankers—well, that can wait too. Good or bad, I don't want to know what's in the letter right now.

My cell phone rings again. It's a call from Kim Peterson, a business associate. Kim is actually more than just a business associate, as we've been doing a "program" together for almost seven years, and normally I'm responsive, but my time in Carmel is like being in heaven, and I don't want to take a chance on being subjected to his aggravation. I decide to let it go to voice mail.

But then I see his text, and the emojis that suggest he's in cardiac arrest.

I call Kim back.

He says, "I just got a subpoena from the SEC. What the fuck is going on?"

"It might be nice, Kim, if you at least started with hello, how are you. I also got a letter from the SEC at the office, but I haven't opened it yet."

Kim says, "I think it's all a big mistake. I think the SEC is confused and has simply misconstrued the legal structure of our liquor-license program. I think there's confusion about a technicality between the loans we're making and the selling of a security, which we certainly do not. I'm sure we can straighten this out."

The program was set up to provide short-term bridge financing for individuals who needed to put money in escrow while they waited for their applications for liquor licenses to be approved by the Department of Alcohol Beverage Control (ABC).

Kim is a fascinating guy. He assumes it's all a mistake, and what I want to say to him is when you get a subpoena from the SEC, it's reasonable to assume that they're not interested in what kind of wine you're serving at dinner.

The subpoena doesn't actually accuse me of anything. It just wants me to gather up some documents and make them available. But I know that getting that subpoena means that time is running out and my plan for the initial public offering (IPO) and for paying everyone back is probably going to be derailed.

I look out into the setting sun over the Pacific Ocean and wonder how a nice Catholic girl from Michigan ended up running a $400 million Ponzi scheme that involves Chicago Title; several San Diego banks; and funds from 250 individual investors in New York, Texas, and China—all in hot pursuit of irrational returns and unmitigated greed.

I close my eyes. Just for the record, the wine I'm drinking is a 1973 Silver Oak.

*** ***

CHAPTER 2

Growing Up

Norman Rockwell is coming to dinner.

I was born in Port Huron, Michigan, in 1965, and was raised in Ann Arbor, where I lived until 1987 when I moved to San Diego. My upbringing was middle class, and I had two loving parents, Daniel and Barbara Champion, who've been married for 50 years. I have a younger half sister, Mia Champion. Our close-knit family ate together every night at 6:00 p.m., which is when dinner is served in the Midwest. Evening discussions focused on world events and business. In the family room, we proudly displayed a complete set of *Encyclopedia Britannica*.

I never really knew my biological father, Ron McMillan. My mother married him when she was 18, and they got divorced six years later when I was just five months old. I didn't see Ron again until I was six years old, when he came to Ann Arbor to approve my legal adoption by my mother's second husband, Dan Champion. I'll leave it to the psychologists to analyze the bonds, the issues, the complexities of fathers and daughters; the divorce; and the impact of all that on my life. No one wants to be abandoned, and all of us want to be loved. I never called Dan my stepfather, though. He was my father in every way, and I will be his daughter forever.

My mom's story is both classic and sad. She'd wanted to attend college, but her parents had other ideas. She was the oldest of four children in a Lebanese Catholic family, and my grandfather was of the very firm opinion that his oldest daughter (my mother) should be married and have children. That was a time when some viewed a woman in college as taking up space that would be better used by a man. So my grandfather threw his daughter an elaborate wedding, and the rest is history.

When the marriage ended in 1971, my mother and I were living in a small apartment in Ann Arbor. My mom called the property management office to report a broken water pipe, and this gorgeous guy, Dan Champion, shows up with a wrench in his hand and his pants completely up to his waist. What more could Mom want?

Dan was putting himself through law school at the University of Michigan, working as the property manager at the apartment complex, and my mom was working as a medical assistant in a doctor's office. Their courtship was short, and they got married later that year.

My mother returned to school at the University of Michigan in 1975. That year she won a Hopwood Award for two nonfiction essays she'd written. First given out in 1931, the Hopwood is awarded to students to "encourage the new, the unusual, and the radical" in creative writing. There have been 3,300 winners, including Arthur Miller, Frank O'Hara, and Marge Piercy, and more than $6 million has been bestowed. I'm proud that my mom graduated in four years with a bachelor's degree in Far Eastern Asian studies. She was a strong female role model and, as a result, I was always driven to succeed.

My parents and my extended family were encouraging, supportive, and loving. There were no drugs or alcohol or abuse, and my home environment reflected the simple mantra: *You can be whatever you want to be.*

I also had a close relationship with Dan's parents. They treated me with genuine love, like I was their own biological granddaughter. They were the sweetest people on earth; I truly loved them and knew that I was part of the family, without question. My grandparents instilled in me a passion for gardening. I loved growing multiple varieties of flowers and had some success with fruits and vegetables, but tomato plants defeated me.

When my probation officer asked me years later, "Is there anything you can point to that happened early in your life to traumatize you?" I thought he was nuts. I had the most normal, loving upbringing. I wasn't pushed hard in school by my parents, and I got *A*'s because that's who I am. The only thing my parents were strict about was coming home every night for dinner. We had to eat our family meal together, which I think is a distinctly midwestern value.

My dad and I played chess regularly. I was on the field hockey team, excelled academically, didn't drink or do drugs in high school, and started working when I was 12. I look at family photos that show what looks like a typical Midwest family, with me smiling, and sporting my trademark long, jet-black hair.

A few years ago I watched the movie *Molly's Game*—in which the true-life protagonist, Molly Bloom, who ran a high-stakes poker game and was later targeted by the FBI—was pushed so hard by her father. That wasn't me. I never had a bad boyfriend and always dated the sweetest guys. Maybe they were a little afraid of me, so there was no pressure to have sex in high school. I was a good girl, and am proud that I waited until a certain age to lose my virginity.

My dad and I are still very close, and until recently, we played chess—we did so online since we lived in different cities—almost every day. My dad teaches me something every time we play. He coaches me at the same time he's kicking my ass. He explains my mistakes but doesn't give me any do-overs, as he's a relentless competitor who likes winning. He's a teacher, and he's always encouraged his daughters to be the best they can be. Until 2020, he won every game that he played with me, so when I finally won a game against him a couple years ago, it was a big deal. My dad is a near grand master, so that victory was the ultimate for me. As time has passed, I now win a few games here and there, but the majority still go to him. He never seems to tire of winning, and I don't like to lose.

Chess teaches you a lot about life—the importance of planning, and playing five moves ahead. And it's never about the move you're making now; it's always about what the board is showing you for the future. So I see life in many ways like a chess match. A battle with rules. And with room for deception.

I've thought a lot about the game over the past seven years, because a Ponzi scheme is very much like chess, in that there's always the possibility of pulling off a win, of escaping the inevitable onslaught of the king. Maybe in the end there could be no exit, but I kept thinking that perhaps someone might accidentally leave the back door unlocked and I could just walk in.

***

Growing up in Ann Arbor meant that University of Michigan football and The Big House (the nickname for Michigan Stadium) were focal points in my college town. My family had season tickets, and I told my parents that I wanted to be the Michigan quarterback when I grew up.

My dad told me that if that were the case, we needed to practice my throwing technique, and he'd make me throw spirals every night. Obviously, when I got older, I realized I was never going to play football for the University of Michigan, but my dad never told me I couldn't do it. He said if that's what I wanted, we could work on it.

In retrospect, I know that the idea of playing football at Michigan wasn't just unrealistic, it was frankly insane, but you can see that early on, I didn't accept limitations, and I assumed I could do everything the boys could.

I've always been driven to succeed, I've always liked being busy, and I'm used to running things. In fact, I think I've been on the run my entire life. I mean, when I say "on the run," I mean being busy, like, I've always worked and gone to school. I've never had the luxury of just studying and partying; even in high school, I always had a job. In fact, as I mentioned above, I started working for my dad at the age of 12.

He managed an enormous apartment complex in Michigan that he was converting into condominiums. And since there was no mail room, I started off in the laundry room, picking up clothes and cleaning the washing machines. Same story all the time—the stuff people leave in the dryer would make your head spin.

It was a large 2,000-unit complex with multiple laundry rooms. In the summers, I also did gardening, or more accurately, mowed the grass and picked up weeds. When I turned 15, my dad put me to work in the leasing office, where I started renting apartments and doing paperwork, such as lease agreements. Many people were surprised to see that I had so much responsibility.

I could certainly multitask. I was a 15-year-old doing my homework, and without missing a beat, telling a young couple that the rent is the rent, we need a security deposit, please fill in this form, sign at the bottom, and give me a check. I loved it.

This was the beginning of my passion for real estate. From collecting rents, I would eventually migrate into development. I wanted to build something. I was a woman in a male-dominated industry, and although I never overtly experienced discrimination, it was still the case that men looked at my breasts and legs before they listened to my brain. It was an old story . . . as well as a current one.

My father was a partner in this first condominium conversion of an apartment complex in the state of Michigan, and I got to sit on his lap, so to speak, and watch the deal-making up close and personal. I liked the wheeling and dealing. I was hooked on the action—and the numbers. Big numbers with lots of zeros. And for a teenager, that was really wild. I didn't actually verbalize my thinking at the time, but in the back of my mind, I wanted to be there someday with plans for my own big numbers.

When I entered my senior year of high school, I got another job. My dad had a buddy who owned one of the title insurance companies in town, and I started doing title insurance research because back then it wasn't like it is now. You actually had to go into the bowels of the county building and look through old map books and research each parcel of land. The owner of the company was trying to assemble large, contiguous parcels of land, and because it was all old farmland, the legal descriptions were like: "The land for farmer Johnson ran from the red barn at the corner of Smith Street to the white picket fence running by the creek 200 yards north of the juniper tree." I got to work with engineers, and frankly, it was all a bit intoxicating.

My dad was trying to do some assemblages with enormous plots of farmland, tie them up, get them zoned, then flip them to his buddy developers to build housing. Same as everybody does today. Nothing new under the sun in that regard.

After graduating from Pioneer High School in Ann Arbor, where I received a "Gold Award" for academic excellence, I attended the University of Michigan. While in college, I continued working at the title insurance office. Not to get too far ahead of the story, but my interaction with these types of companies will prove to be pretty damn interesting. And I liked working, so I got another job as an assistant administrator at a law firm.

My goal was to attend law school. Since my evenings were free, I also took a job at night as the front-desk girl at a tanning salon while I did my homework. Despite this demanding schedule, I graduated from Michigan in four years as a "Regents-Alumni Scholar." I did find time to have fun—I loved attending football games and learned to drink beer and date boys.

That's how I've been my whole life. I've never just sat back, and I've always loved being busy. But I have a very short attention span, which is a problem for me. You know, my husband is a guy who can sit and do one thing and be very focused. That's why he's such a good golfer. I, on the other hand, am always thinking about a hundred other things while I'm hanging over the ball.

The complete truth is, I've always worked hard because I like working and like accomplishing things, but I've also always liked money. I've talked to wealthy guys along the way who've told me that they simply loved their work and it was never about the money. *Bullshit.* It's *always* about the money. And when is enough, enough? Maybe the day before you die, but otherwise, never. It's how you keep score.

During the almost seven-year run of the program, I took in about $60 million for my own account. I used it to buy real estate, including a few vacation homes; built restaurants; opened retail shops; and supported 800 employees. I put most of the money into those deals. I had one car, a Range Rover, which I needed for the dogs, but otherwise, I just didn't do much of the luxury thing.

After graduating from Michigan in 1987 with a major in political science and philosophy, I decided to move to San Diego to attend California Western School of Law. It was an easy decision. I looked at their promotional video with the ocean, the sand, the sailboats on the bay, volleyball players on the beach, surfers with their boards at the Hotel del Coronado, and then I looked out my window at the snow. A no-brainer.

In addition, I liked San Diego's location, on the border with Mexico. I wanted a more global view of the world, more than just my little pod in the Midwest. And, of course, after spending 22 winters in Michigan, there was a certain appeal to the idea of not freezing my ass off in February.

My parents didn't want me to go; in fact, my dad didn't speak to me for six months. He thought Southern California was the land of fruits and nuts. But I was fortunate that I'd know at least one person when I arrived in San Diego.

My date to the high school senior prom was Kenny Cain. We didn't have a romantic relationship; we were just friends who needed a date, and we stayed in touch. When Kenny learned that I was moving to San Diego, he suggested I call his older brother, Steve, who was already living there. Steve had also grown up in Ann Arbor, having graduated from the same high school as I had three years earlier. Steve's parents were both professors at the University of Michigan. There was no way he could go to a school where he had a high likelihood of returning from the bar after a few beers and running into his mom on campus. The die was cast—Steve was going to attend Michigan State.

Steve graduated and got a job in San Diego working in the furniture-manufacturing industry. Two years later, when I was heading west, his younger brother called Steve and told him that this nice girl was coming to San Diego and would he do him a favor and show her around for a few days.

I called Steve and said, "I'm coming on August 11th, and I'm staying at the Howard Johnson's on El Cortez Hill [near downtown San Diego]."

Steve replied, "Great. I'll pick you up and take you to dinner."

I landed, got to the hotel, and then before my date with Steve, I took a bus across the Coronado Bridge, hiked up my dress, and walked into the ocean in front of the Hotel del Coronado. Water up to my knees. Sun setting. That day was the start of the rest of my life.

Steve took me to dinner at the Chart House overlooking the ocean. I loved the salad bar, and I remember that he had a gin and tonic, and I had a Heineken. We sat in the bar area and talked about all our friends back home. And that began my life and love affair with not only Steve Cain, but also San Diego.

The next day my mother called to ask how the evening with Steve had gone. I was very clear. I said, "I don't think he likes me very much, but I'm going to marry him someday." I've always been relentless in my pursuit of a goal.

We were married three years later to the day I landed in San Diego— August 11, 1990. I was 23 years old.

*** ***

CHAPTER 3

From Basement
to Boardroom

I took the steps, since the elevator was
out of order.

From 1988 to 1997, I worked my way up the ladder in the
male-dominated world of San Diego real estate. San Diego was
growing—currently it is the eighth-largest city in the U.S. The
region was becoming a center for tech and biotech, the military and
the defense industries were vital, the blighted downtown was being
redeveloped, the binational economy with Mexico was growing, and
tourism continued to boom. All aspects of real estate—industrial,
commercial, and residential—were prospering, and I saw a lot of
wealth being created. I was definitely focused on making money, and
I thought that real estate was the way to do it.

I started at ConAm, a large property management company with
several thousand units in their portfolio. When I joined, they were
actively working with the Resolution Trust Corporation (RTC) on
fixing and liquidating problem real estate assets from the savings-and-
loan debacle earlier in the decade.

The company CEO was Dan Epstein, a smart, powerful, well-respected leader in the real estate industry, and I wanted him to be my mentor. But my first job was to just get in the door, and I had enough chutz-pah to talk my way in, starting as an assistant to an assistant, with my first desk located in the basement. I did the basic grunt work in the apartment management division, which amounted to not much more than collecting rents and trying to keep tenants happy.

The "mail room" was okay for a while, but I had a clear plan and goal: I was going to get into the meetings that were taking place in the conference room on the top floor, where the deals were being made, and where the game pieces on the Monopoly board were being moved around.

I wanted to pick the brains of the best in the business—without them knowing they'd been picked. All I needed was an elegant, simple, devious plan. The company was filled with nice white men, and let's face it, they were suckers for long legs and cookies, and I had both. That is, I could bake. After all, for a midwestern girl who went to football games in cold weather, this was a no-brainer. So I baked cookies and left them in strategic places. It was simple—I just had to lure the bears out from their dens into the open, where I could get a clean shot at them.

At the time, Epstein had an executive vice president, Mike Dorazio, and he was the bear I was gunning for. I was charming, witty, and I could talk sports. I knew a golf ball from a hockey puck, and I could discuss who was going first in the NFL draft and whether the Chargers needed a new wide-out or a middle linebacker.

So one day I left the basement, cornered Dorazio at the water cooler, and suggested to him that a man of his standing needed his own assistant. Why was he sharing an assistant with another executive when he clearly had enough work to warrant his own? After all, I told him that a man of his distinction and executive skill should *not* have to share an assistant with Dan Epstein, the CEO. Ultimately, I was aiming for the biggest bear, but I needed to bag Junior first.

I told Mike that I was just the girl he needed. He was a lawyer, and I'd just finished one year of law school at the University of San Diego. Also, I could spell the word *legal*, followed by those two important words: *Sue 'em*. I told him that we were made for each other, and then, of course, all those cookies would be his alone.

Dorazio was the head of syndications at ConAm, and this was a critical component for me going forward. I wanted to learn the rules for various types of real estate offerings and how to structure deals with outside investors. Dorazio was only too happy to take a poke at his boss, and the next week, I was moved up to the second floor as his assistant. At least now I was on the right floor, but still in the wrong pew. The conference room I wanted was around the corner, down the hall. A pitching wedge at most.

Fortunately, my desk was directly across from CEO Dan Epstein's door. So when I went in to see my boss, I had to walk right by his office. If you're hunting bear, you need to be armed with quality ammunition. I put a large bowl of M&Ms on the corner of my desk, next to the plate of chocolate-chip cookies. This was almost going to be too easy.

Still, sitting outside the conference room is not the same as sitting inside. I needed Plan B.

Dorazio was impressed with my work ethic and attention to detail and complimented me over the next few months. One evening he took me out for a drink, and I realized that this was the time to break out the bear-spray perfume. I suggested to him, with impeccable logic, and after two martinis, that I could be even more valuable to him if I were by his side in the meetings—listening, taking notes, and supporting him. Dorazio liked that idea.

Sure, there was a bit of flirting, but I never let any man cross the line. I was always charming. Two drinks and home to Steve.

And then at the next Monday-morning management meeting, Dorazio walked in with me right behind him. Epstein said, "Why is *she* in this meeting?"

Dorazio stiffened his spine and said, "I want her here. She'll add value."

Epstein did pause for a moment, considering his options, but he waved us both in, and from then on, I would do anything for Dan Epstein. He became my mentor, and I've been eternally grateful for that.

But it was still a male-chauvinist world, and as I maneuvered through it, I had to continually duck and dodge the offers of "Why don't you come up and see my etchings; I have an extra toothbrush."

I began to work with Dorazio on troubled real estate assets that had been taken over by the RTC. This was after the financial crisis caused by the deregulation of the financial industry, and there were distressed properties all over the country. I proved to be very adept at the negotiations with owners and lenders. It was all workouts and liquidations, and there were plenty of sharp elbows because there was never enough money to make everyone whole.

I was moving up, but I wasn't quite ready to go out on my own.

After I finished that first year of law school, I came to the conclusion that lots of first-year students come to: I didn't want to be a lawyer. I liked deals, but I knew that I needed more experience, so I transferred to the University of San Diego business school, where I earned an MBA.

The reason many people go to business school is not to learn business or accounting or discounted cash flow; they go to meet the other students who are there to learn those things. And so that's what I did. The savings-and-loan debacle had created a demand for asset managers and work-out specialists (professionals who identify the causes of problem loans), but there was a shortage of experienced companies in that area. It turned out that several of my second-year classmates had been recruited by one of the largest companies. They respected my work and they needed people, so I got on the boat with them and rode it to shore.

After graduation, I took a job with the Walters Management Company, which had a deep portfolio of RTC properties that needed solutions. One of their high-profile problem assets was The Promenade, a two-story, beach-area retail center. Too much debt, too optimistic about the rents, over budget on the renovations—a classic shit show.

Walters took the case, and I got to be the lead dog on the sled. We got rid of certain tenants, added new ones, did some renovation, opened it up a little, added signage, and when it was done, I used that workout as the thesis for my MBA. We sold it and got back most of the dough for the RTC, but in the end, second-floor retail is a dead man walking. People in Southern California do not like to walk upstairs.

I was ambitious. I wanted more and bigger action, and I didn't want to just be cleaning up someone else's mess. I wanted to *develop*.

***

Next stop, the Koll Company, a multibillion-dollar real estate development operation headquartered in Orange County, owned by one man, Don Koll. The Koll Company had developed or acquired more than 150 million square feet of industrial, office, retail, resort, and golf courses. I'd just landed a job at the real estate equivalent of Goldman Sachs, and I was ready to rock 'n' roll. But I knew there was one piece of this puzzle that was going to be a problem for me.

In the real estate business, a few considerations lurk in the mind of any entrepreneur—that is: "If I can do this for Jones, why can't I do this for myself?" And one of the major limiting factors in the real estate racket is access to capital. You can tie up a piece of land; and you might have the brains to design the project, understand the market, and get the approvals, but to really get the deal done, you're going to need someone with a net-worth statement and a willingness to sign on a construction loan or a mortgage and be your partner. Don Koll did not need partners.

Ownership is a constant tension that lives in every partnership: How much do the brains get, and how much does the money get? For now, I had to work for someone else, but my plan was that this was only an interlude before I started my own company. I was going to play Annie to Don Koll's Daddy Warbucks . . . for now.

If you wanted to succeed as a woman at Koll in Orange County, you needed to look the part of a Koll girl, and that meant St. John knit suits with padded shoulders, and other clothing from Nordstrom's. That was my uniform.

Early in my time at Koll, I was handed a problem child: the almost-empty La Jolla Village Square retail center that had been built as an indoor luxury center and now was almost empty and needed a complete makeover. My assignment was to resuscitate the patient currently on life support, perform open-heart surgery, and then get it back online, making money for the owners.

The initial renovation plans presented to the community were reject-ed outright—in fact, it bordered on hostile rebellion with a touch of armed insurrection. Koll was planning a discount-store mall with retailers like Ross and Marshalls, and the La Jolla community (the second-wealthiest zip code in San Diego) was thinking differently. They wanted to "open it up" and bring in more upscale tenants, not just more of the same.

City permits were on hold, a stalemate at hand. The first meeting that I attended was in a hotel ballroom with 300 angry residents anxious to express their thoughts. After I introduced myself, I could see some folks in the back beginning to figuratively light torches.

No one from Koll—none of the executives—bothered to attend this meeting. All those white shirts and blue suits and BMWs in the Orange County parking lot were somehow missing in action on that evening.

Their vision for the project was flawed, and I felt like the point guy in Vietnam, trying to avoid stepping on a field of punji stakes.

I was supposed to give the community an update on the mall's progress and where we were with the city approvals. The men on the community-planning group were raising their voices to me, and the rest of the audience was periodically joining in and egging them on.

I was supposed to sell them a bill of goods, provide a bit of misdirection, pull the permits, and get out of Dodge. That is *not* what happened.

I kept telling them about all the good things that were coming, and they kept seeing the double hustle. Finally, the meeting reached a stalemate. There was nothing more to be accomplished that night, so I headed home to lick my wounds, and wondered what to say to my bosses.

As I was walking to my car, local city councilmember Harry Mathis walked over to me. I was pretty beat-up and depressed. Mathis was a wise and seasoned politician.

In a caring way, he gave me some well-worn political advice that I've always remembered. He told me that when the community says you fucked up, your best approach is to say, yes, I understand, you're right, and I agree to listen better.

He called it the "You're right, I'm wrong, and I'm going to fix it, Mr. Community Member" rule for real estate development. And that evening turned out to be one of the defining moments of my career.

The next day I was called into an emergency meeting at the construction-site trailer. All the men I worked for, including real estate icon Eli Broad, had heard about the meeting and were visibly upset. They wanted to know how this meeting had gone so badly. They'd given me a chance, and in their minds, I'd let them down. The Koll team was angry, and I thought that I'd be fired. I looked like I might be heading back to the tanning salon. But if that were the case, then I wasn't going down without taking a few swings of my own. There was nothing to lose, no reason to sugarcoat anything, so I looked directly at the group.

I told them, "You designed a lousy project, the community hates it, you wanted me to shove it down their throats, and that is not going to happen. You need to go back to the drawing board. You guys are all gutless wonders the way you've run this project. You've hidden your collective heads in the sand and have been unwilling to listen to the community. You figured you could bulldoze everyone and then slink away in the dark of night. And then you trotted this nice little girl out to take the arrows meant for you. Not going to happen. No fucking way."

And then I just stood there. There was the classic long pause, and then one of the most senior executives stood up and simply said, "Thank you. We will support you. Now go make it right."

The next day in the construction office, one of the top lieutenants stopped me at the door and said, "I only have one thing to say: I'm glad you don't carry a gun."

And fix it I did. The La Jolla Village Square project was one of my most successful ventures; it put me on the map and made me famous in San Diego real estate circles. The project became an iconic grand slam, and Koll made me the face of their development. I was featured in the newspaper and on TV, and was interviewed for real estate journals. This only whetted my appetite for more and bigger projects. Like in the *Little Shop of Horrors*: "Feed me."

When the mall was about to be sold, community leaders asked Koll to leave me in charge of management services going forward. A cartoon in the *La Jolla Light* newspaper showed a big pair of shoes representing Koll, and me standing in them. I'm quoted in the article: "I told Farallon Capital [the new owner] that the most important part of this deal is to make sure they're in tune with the community needs and wants. That's the bottom line because the community members are the patrons and customers of the mall. They should never forget that."

To succeed at Koll as a woman, you had to look and dress the part; and you had to be smarter, craftier, more relentless, and yes, perhaps even more devious than all the men in the room. It was a blood sport, and I wanted to play at the highest level. I wanted to show them that I could do it without sleeping my way to the top. I wouldn't take any crap. I'd been underestimated by them once, and that was never going to happen again.

But as my role expanded, I was being asked to spend more time at the main office in Newport Beach, away from my home, the beach, my dogs, and my husband, Steve. Trade-offs needed to be made. Stick it out, with a slow slog of certainty; or pick up my skirt, wade into the deep water, and tell them to pound sand.

This was 1997, and only a few executive real estate women were running their own shops and doing their own deals. I had no role models to look to for guidance. I had to figure out on my own if I could play with the big boys—whether in the boardroom or on the golf course. I knew that I was smart enough, and to be honest, fair or not, I'had one more advantage in dealing with this male-dominated world: I'd been told my whole life that I was drop-dead gorgeous. I was always going to get a second look . . . even if I didn't get a second chance.

*** ***

CHAPTER 4
Playing Golf

*"The most important shot in golf is the
next one."* —Ben Hogan

I learned to play golf because it was good for business. A lot of men in finance and real estate development played, and it was a great way to get to know them. I can hit the ball far for a lady. The guys were always surprised and impressed when I stepped up to the tee and whacked the ball. I wore the cutest golf outfits—those little dresses that just covered your butt. And I'd work it when I was playing with the men, which was most of the time.

And then when it came to those member-guest-scramble tournaments and I got to drive from the women's tee box, well, I sure was in demand by those guys.

You play golf to network and make deals; hitting the ball is just one small element of the game. In 1994, Steve and I joined the Farms Golf Club in Rancho Santa Fe, a wealthy enclave in north San Diego County. The Farms wasn't a classic country club; it had no tennis, no pool, no dinners—nothing except 18 magnificent holes with a slope rating of 145, which means it was a very challenging course, and also why it attracted people who wanted to play golf and do nothing more.

I was always a good athlete, and I picked up the game quickly. For my first real round of golf at the Farms, I was paired with Lance Allworth, who'd been a famous wide receiver for the San Diego Chargers. They called him "Bambi." For my next round, I was paired with my husband, Steve, and I got a hole-in-one on the second hole, a 129-yard, par 3. I joined the Farms women's golf team, where I was a desired partner and thoroughly enjoyed the competition—when I wasn't busy working.

Steve was a good golfer. He played serious golf with the big boys, and when they did the couples "Save your marriage" golf games on Sunday afternoons, we were contenders and won frequently.

A crossroad in my career was coming. I had a great job at Koll, but an hour commute was part of the deal. Steve was still working for the family furniture business, and his daily commute was to Tijuana, Mexico (just south of San Diego). By 1997, we'd bought a beautiful home in the Mission Hills neighborhood, an older community close to downtown and the airport. Along with our three dogs and a view of the ocean from our patio, we were beginning to live the dream.

I'd grown tired of traveling the freeway, though. I'd spent the last ten years making other people rich, and I was ready to be my own boss. No matter how well I was being paid, it was usually to dig other people out of their messes. Now was *my* time. At least if there were going to be messes, they would be of my own making.

At about the same time, Steve decided he'd had enough of the "family business," and he was ready to spread his entrepreneurial chops as well. As I said, golf is only an excuse to network, so one Saturday morning, Steve met a guy named John McNeil. McNeil had made some money and was looking for his next big thing. He cared about the environment and sustainability, and he'd developed some technology for a molded pulp product for packaging, much better than the white popcorn that was being used to cushion products at that time.

McNeil was the consummate, charismatic salesman. Steve, more modest in style and detail oriented, was strong in operations, and by the time they got to the third hole (par 5, over water, #1 handicap), they'd hatched a plan. John would get the contracts; Steve would deliver the nuts and bolts. They launched Pacific Pulp Molding in 1997, and their partnership has continued to this day.

I didn't know it at the time, but a dozen years later, I would meet a golfer at the Farms named Kim Peterson. We chatted up a deal, and he became a key part of my life. I'm profoundly sorry that I ever met him.

Steve and I were two people about to leave phenomenal corporate jobs where we were being well paid, both deciding to go out on our own at the same time, which was insane. But we didn't have any children, we had a house that was paid for, and we owned our cars free and clear (and we drove them until they collapsed). No credit-card debt, no student loans. What the hell—there's never a really good time to risk it all, but this time seemed as good as any!

***

I was going into real estate development, so the first thing I'd need, after having my head examined, was a name. I had a couple weeks left at Koll, and one particular day I was in Pasadena at the Ritz-Carlton having drinks and smoking cigars with some of the guys on one of the projects. One dirty martini in, I posed the problem that "if" I were going to start something, what should I call it?

One of the men said, "You have to sound like you've got a powerhouse behind you, because if you want to play in commercial real estate development, sweetie, at the moment no women work there." The other guy took a napkin and wrote the name American National Investments, which sounded big enough to me. And then he drew a simple logo. End of story, or the beginning, depending on your point of view. Four glasses of red wine, two dirty gin martinis, and I was in business. On the way out, the other guy says, "What about putting 'International' in front, but we all agreed that would have been overreaching a bit. But one more round . . . and maybe.

I saved that napkin for more than 20 years, but when the receiver appointed by the SEC came in with an order to clean out the files and documents from my office, one of the movers simply threw it in the trash, along with some other stuff in the drawer. Nothing more than a napkin, but it's the kind of thing that haunts a woman's soul.

I read a quote by French novelist Honoré de Balzac when I was in law school: "Behind every great fortune lies a great crime." Who knows why that came up back then. . . .

*** ***

CHAPTER 5

House of Blues

Homeless people also like music.

During the renovation of La Jolla Village Square, I'd met a real estate broker named John Beaney. This fellow was famous in his field, as he was the national representative doing all the negotiating for large-space tenants in major shopping malls such as Ross Dress for Less, TJ Maxx, and Crown Books. He knew everyone you needed to know, and as you might suspect, he took a liking to me. After all, I had a shopping center, and he had tenants. It was what you might call in Yiddish, a *shidduch*, meaning "a match made in heaven." We made a couple of deals, the project was successful, and that only served to motivate me even more to go out on my own.

It's not so easy to do so in the real estate business, though. Lots of pieces need to come together to get something built, particularly when it's your first time as the developer, not an employee. And as I've noted previously, this was not an industry that was used to seeing women in hard hats.

You can't even start dancing until you tie up a piece of dirt or a building. What I mean by that is you can't just hang up a shingle that says "Real Estate Developer—come on in and have a seat." And the tricky part is that you need to have the *right* to do a deal, to get your hands on a deal long enough to figure out if you even really have a deal worth doing. You need to tie something up tight enough to control it, but not so tight that you can't bail out of the project without forfeiting a ton of money—when you find out that it doesn't pencil.

It's the cost of the pencil that can kill you at times, and here's how: First, you tie up something, which means some legal fees and probably some option payments. Sometimes those payments are refundable, but most of the time you have to "go hard" with some dough. Now you have some real money at risk. Next, the clock starts to tick, but trust me, you don't need a Vacheron Constantin to keep time. That deadline—when you have to go or not go, put up real money and close—is immutable, and you'll mark it on your calendar in red.

Okay, so now you have a deal that you're feeling good about. The next dance step is a tango. First, you hustle around to see if you can get all the regulatory approvals and determine who in the community is opposed—that is, do you have an "as-of-right" project, or do you have to go into begging mode? At the same time, you've hired an architect to draw a fantasy picture of what it could be—complete with parks, jobs, affordable housing, and tax increments. You fully understand that this picture can't be built for any rational amount of money, but you're going to show the governmental decision makers visions of sugarplums, and if you can get a yes, then as you move along down the road, you can delete the plums, substitute apples, and begin to "value-engineer" it, which is code for cutting out all the stuff that was sexy and expensive and putting back in stuff that is basic but affordable.

And while you're dancing, you need to find money; you need to secure an investor. You need to run the numbers in such a way that real money is willing to join in. You have to find the balance between optimistic potential and unvarnished reality.

And then don't forget about that clock ticking down and the calendar on the wall. As the option gets closer to its expiration, you need to go back to the seller and beg for more time; and the seller, who's losing patience, has to consider whether to pull the plug and start over with another developer and risk litigation (legitimate or not) or hang on, giving one more extension, which of course requires making an additional option payment.

All the while, you're still looking for the real money. You're trying to sell the guy a House of Blues, and he's thinking that all you have is a house of cards. And then some other developer shows up after you've done all the work and almost have it figured out, and he goes to the seller and whispers in his ear that he'll pay more and close faster.

So the seller thinks he has a better offer and wants his property back— he wants to tell you to die and pound sand. Back to the lawyers to read the fine print on the option agreement. More money.

There's a disagreement of sorts. Now you go to the escrow company. They're the ones holding the money, and the seller wants your money and his property back. But you want the property, so whatever happens, do *not* release any of your money. You refuse to sign the release of funds, finding excuses and sending some meaningless threats so you don't lose your deposit. More lawyers.

And then as you get ready to close, the seller extracts one last pound of flesh; while at the same time, like a Penn and Teller magic trick, the money finally shows up, the project gets its approvals, and although you're outraged at being leveraged by the seller, you take the deal because you're already down a deep rabbit hole, and there's only one way out the other side. And, what the hell, at least you're going to live to fight another day, and maybe those crazy rents that you projected—who knows, maybe they'll show up as well. And that problem is certainly for a later day. But at this point, you are now formally known as a "developer."

***

I didn't have anything lined up yet, but I had Beaney. I was doing the double straddle. While I was at Koll, I was working with Beaney to find a way for my escape. It's the classic trapeze move. You don't want to let go of your swing until you have a reasonable shot at grabbing on to the one coming your way. Timing on that one is everything. If you let go too early, no trapeze; if you let go too late, you hope to hell there's a net.

Koll kept pushing me to move up to Orange County, but that wasn't going to happen. Steve's business was in Tijuana, and the commuting distance—both of us going in opposite directions—would destroy our marriage, so the Rubicon was getting closer and closer.

All over the country, urban cores were being revitalized, and I saw enormous potential in downtown San Diego. It would have a dense urban fabric with street-level retail and housing above. I could see the future of my city, and I could see my *own* future.

As my first project, I chose the old Woolworth building. It sat on a full city block, 60,000 square feet, between 5th and 6th, Broadway and C Street. Woolworth, started in 1879, originated the concept of the "five-and-dime" stores, the predecessor to chains such as Walmart and Costco. But the company hadn't adapted to the modern age of retailing, and it was selling off its precious real estate.

At that time, the San Diego Woolworth building was empty, only occupied by the homeless, the drug addicted, and the lost souls of downtown—none of whom were paying rent. The British parent company was ready to toss in the towel. And Beaney was holding the towel rack.

The operating principle for a fledgling developer with no money is to select a property that no one really wants. After all, if the property is obviously terrific, someone with real money would buy it. The first trick is to see future value in what others won't waste their time or money on. But the real trick is to get someone else to share that vision.

Beaney had been engaged to sell *all* of the remaining 400 U.S. Woolworth sites. They were closing their American presence, and the British owners weren't inclined to sell them off in onesies and twosies. They wanted a package bulk buyer. The problem is that I only wanted *one* building.

Remember the cookies with Con Am and Dan Epstein? Well, I went back to the oven. I found out that Beaney's birthday was coming up the following week, so naturally I decided to bake him something. Three slices of German chocolate cake and two martinis later, Beaney and I were beginning to come to an understanding.

He oversaw the whole portfolio, but I explained to him that San Diego was a provincial blah-blah on the edge of nowhere, and no one would want this one location, so why not sell it to me—I gave him that vision. I sold him smoke and mirrors and those damn sugarplums (they'd gone up in price since then). And I gave him another piece of cake.

And then I had control of one block of downtown San Diego.

***

Now the next thing I needed besides money was an anchor tenant. Who could I find that would want to be in that location? I needed someone credible who would pay rent or at least be the anchor tenant so that I could get other people interested and then could get this thing financed. I call this finding the nexus between opportunity and desire.

I'd met the House of Blues owners, Isaac Tigrett and Dan Aykroyd, in Los Angeles while working with Koll on the Tokyo Olympics. All I had to do was convince the owners that their next stop needed to be San Diego. Bring Hollywood sex and music to the corner of Sixth and C. Like the Blues Brothers band, I was on a mission from God. I met with Liam Thornton, the leasing representative for the House of Blues, and spun a tale of downtown renovation, of young people hungry for music. Liam went down like a stone, believing that even though the location was "marginal at best," he could sell it to his bosses as "edgy."

The House of Blues already had the Anaheim/Disney location about to open, and they had the original West Hollywood venue, so of course every stool needs a third leg—downtown San Diego. Cue Adele, opening first act. And poof in a cloud of white smoke; the deal was done.

Now at that moment, the truth is, I still had nothing, but I had more nothing than I had ever had before. From this point forward, it was just skiing downhill and don't hit any trees.

I had land, I had a tenant, I had buzz, and the only thing left was to get the money. And as I told you, that's exactly when it just shows up.

My major investor in the project was an Orange County guy named Stan Hanson, whom I'd met through a friend. That's a running theme in my adventure—you had to know someone who knew someone you needed to know.

He became enamored of the project and of me, and he invested $2 million as the original equity. I combined that with a long-term lease from the House of Blues, and that was enough to secure the construction financing. Break ground, newspaper articles, flashbulbs, and hey, I finally got me a hard hat with my name on it.

The House of Blues got built, it opened, and it was a smashing success.

But after the champagne; the ribbon cutting; and the sex, drugs, and rock 'n' roll, it's time for the third act of the play to unfold, the one where the true nature of the actors emerges, the absolute sine qua non for big projects with big egos attached. With appropriate attribution to Hamlet, "Real estate development, thy name is litigation."

Hanson had a friend, Steve Rebeil. Rebeil went to Hanson and uttered the most famous of all lines: "This deal isn't big enough for the three of us." Last I looked, there weren't three of us in this deal, but Rebeil wanted to buy me out, or more accurately, push me out and take my share.

I wasn't interested in selling, so there was clearly a disconnect. I waged the war, I got it financed, I got it built, I stood at the front door in a short black dress on opening night and danced with Dan Aykroyd, and so tell me, in what universe do you think I'm a seller?

They wanted what I had, so there were only two ways to get it. One, you could try to buy my share from me; or two, you could simply try to steal it. They picked the second. And how exactly did they do it? The two men made me disappear with the stroke of a pen. They forged a grant deed, using a friendly title-and-escrow officer. One day I had 50 percent, and the next day I had zero. Gone girl.

But I wasn't going quietly into the night, so I went to see Hanson.

There's something about those moments when a powerful man is confronted by a strong woman with a definitive claim about his bad behavior—whether it's sexual harassment, physical abuse, or simple thievery—that brings out the testosterone and energizes the confrontation. Hanson had a big office, a nice desk, a view of Newport Harbor, and this little girl with the long black hair is sitting in front of him, suggesting that he's acted badly and that she'd like him to recant his sins and put things back the way they should be.

Hanson said to me, "Are you out of your fucking mind? No fucking way. See me in court? You'll never win. I'll bury you in legal fees. You'll be an old, crippled crone living in a homeless shelter before you ever see another dime from me"—or words to that effect.

Shakespeare, in *Henry VI*, says, "Let's kill all the lawyers," but I wasn't going to do that before I could hire an attorney to sue the two men who tried to steal from me. What Shakespeare neglected to mention was that most lawyers want to be paid for their time, unless you can find one who'll take your case on contingency, effectively willing to roll the dice for a better payday rather than an hourly rate.

I knew the Mike Kirby law firm. The attorneys there were young and hungry, and there was a lawyer there named Jim Lance whom I convinced to take the case on contingency. Look, I thought it was a slam-dunk case, but lawyers will tell you that there's no such thing. The firm took a big risk on me, and just as Hanson said he would, he played hardball. Depositions and demands.

There were many twists in the litigation, but toward the end of the case, it looked like I was going to come up empty. We couldn't find the smoking gun. And then, just like in the movies, there was that unexpected twist.

A well-known axiom is that there's no honor among thieves. And as the screw turned, the House of Blues was even more profitable than they'd ever thought possible. Hanson came to the conclusion that one con wasn't enough, so he doubled down and decided to screw his would-be partner, Rebeil, as well.

All it would take is some more forged documents and he'd have a shot at keeping 100 percent of the project for himself. Rebeil discovered this maneuver at the last minute and realized that he could end up with nothing, so he decided that one good deed deserved another.

We were at the courthouse steps, ready to go in and see the judge, and Rebeil showed up with a stack of papers, walked up to Lance, and handed them to him. They were the forged documents.

That's how you win a million dollars. You rely on the kindness of strangers.

I almost got cheated out of my first signature real estate development because two men had a friend at the title/escrow company who agreed to forge a signature. You can't make this stuff up.

And as for Mike Kirby, well, he'll show up later in my life. Just wait and see.

*** ***

CHAPTER 6

A Basic Primer on Liquor-License Loans

Hey, how does a guy get a drink around here?

I learned how one goes about getting a liquor license in the State of California while I was working on the House of Blues project. I didn't know it at the time, but this experience proved to be very important to me a few years later. The guy that helped us get that license was an attorney, Bill Adams. He was the absolute go-to guy for licenses. As fate would have it, I would be contacting him for my own account in a few years.

California has a rather unique, obtuse, backward, arbitrary, arcane, and ripe-for-corruption liquor-license application process. If you want to serve booze in California—in a restaurant, café, bar, or bodega—you'll need a liquor license. The process is ostensibly clear, but it lends itself at times to being unreasonably opaque and political. I think the majority of applicants would liken it to Lombard Street in the fog and the rain in San Francisco.

A short primer in California from the website License Locators:

"In California, liquor licenses are distributed by the Department of Alcohol Beverage Control. This process can be difficult and time-consuming; as licenses are limited within the state of California, finding a seller willing to part with their license for a fair price can be a challenging endeavor. New business owners must often privately purchase their required alcohol permits from a pool of proprietors who possess a pre-existing license."

So far, so good. But the big one is next—the absolute, nonnegotiable element of getting a liquor license in California is the requirement for an escrow. An escrow essentially is a lockbox where various parties put in things including money; it's a safe place, and when all the requirements have been met, someone unlocks the box. An escrow should hold the various crown jewels in a neutral and fair way, and it should be administered by someone above suspicion, like a title company—Chicago Title, for example.

But, of course, if someone unlocks the box early, then when someone else goes to get what is supposed to be *in* the box, they, unfortunately, will find that the box is empty. In this case, unlike a safe-deposit box, it will turn out that more than one person in the program has a set of keys.

See the info below from the Alcoholic Beverage Consulting Service:

Escrow Requirements

"If there is any purchase price or consideration in connection with the transfer of a business operated under a retail license, an escrow must be established with some person, corporation, or association not a party to the transfer before the filing of such transfer with the Department of the Alcoholic Beverage Control Act. The full amount of the purchase price or consideration must be placed in escrow. Escrow agreements must provide for payment only after the transfer of the license is approved by this Department. Section 24074.3 requires that the applicant, within 30 days of application, furnish the Department a statement, under penalty of perjury, that the purchase price or consideration has been deposited with the escrow holder. The applicant shall also submit a copy to the transferor and a copy to the escrow holder. In this connection, a misrepresentation may be grounds for denial."

The big idea here is that you need to show the ABC that you had the dough already, good to go, up front, in a safe place. Otherwise, you could get an approval, and then after the fact, race around and try to get the money to pay for the license, or try to flip the license or hustle the seller of the license or maneuver. And the ABC wanted to try to eliminate that potential maneuvering by requiring the deposit up front. There was no room for J. Wellington Wimpy: "I'll gladly pay you Tuesday for a hamburger today." And as we all know, Tuesday never comes.

More on Liquor Licenses

There are basically five different types of liquor licenses. They vary based on the venue and what you're selling (hard liquor versus beer and wine, serving food or not, music or not, and so on); but regardless, whatever license you seek, you'll need an escrow agreement and an escrow holder when you're trying to secure the right to sell alcohol in California.

It is precisely at this point in the story where we need to meet Chicago Title Insurance, a major escrow company in San Diego. Chicago Title is owned by Fidelity National Financial, Inc. (NYSE), whose revenue last year was approximately $8.6 billion, and the company has a current market capitalization of approximately $11.4 billion. This is important because that many billions will later definitely qualify them for what people look to when they're unhappy and want to find someone to give them their money back—otherwise known as "deep pockets." And deep pockets are what you need to find when you go looking for the money you thought was somewhere, but isn't there anymore and has gone somewhere else—or it's just gone.

During my career up to that point, I'd done numerous real estate transactions and had used Chicago Title for all of them. For example, Chicago Title had done all the title and escrow work for the House of Blues. So I was a known quantity in their office at the corner of 7th and B Street in downtown San Diego.

The ABC requirement is that you post the *full amount* of the consideration for the liquor license into the escrow until the transaction closes. This means that the money is tied up and can't be used to develop the property, buy furniture and fixtures, pay the lawyers, and so on. And unless you're a deep-pocketed restaurateur (or a major corporation like the House of Blues), you probably don't have enough money to tie up $100,000 to $350,000 for a hard-to-get Type 48 license that allows you to operate a bar or nightclub without having to sell food, so you go looking to borrow that money.

You need to find someone who can find someone who will lend you some patient (albeit expensive) money on your behalf; let it sit in a nice, safe escrow just long enough to get approved for the liquor license; and then the applicant replaces that "bridge" loan with his own money and can start selling Bloody Marys.

The investor puts the money in an account at an escrow company—for example, Chicago Title. Then the escrow company fills out a Form 226 that tells the ABC that they have some money in the name of Bob Smith, and that money sits there sits there until Mr. Smith's application is granted, at which time Smith puts in his own money to pay back the investors who lent him the money during the application process, and the seller of the license gets his money, and the deal closes. In the middle, the investors who made the loan for Mr. Smith get back their original investment, along with some fees and interest in exchange for putting up the money for the applicant. A discussion on the precise amount of fees and interest will be for a later date.

On the other hand, if the license isn't approved, then the money in the escrow is returned to the investor, and the escrow is abandoned. From the investor's standpoint, his only real economic loss is the time/value of his money with respect to another potential investment.

When you strip away all the fuzz, the process offers a substantial profit-making potential if you can figure out the system. Basically, you get to lend money at high interest rates to someone who needs the money so he can get a license to sell liquor in his establishment, and he doesn't get his hands on the license until he pays you back. What could be simpler?

As to whether opening a bar or restaurant is a good idea, I will leave that for a future discussion as well.

*** ***

CHAPTER 7

My First Restaurant

What started as a lament ended up on Lamont.

I f you're a real estate developer, the financial recession of 2008–2009 was brutal. Values had plummeted, and no one was making new deals. Financial institutions and other lenders were simply feasting on the carcasses that were littered across the country. I didn't have the patience or the capital to be a buy-and-hold investor. I was looking for opportunities that I could develop or redevelop, and then, of course, I'd need to find the capital to do the project. But after the House of Blues, I had a good reputation, and I wanted to do my own deals.

A real estate broker called me up and wanted to show me a property at 4437 Lamont Street. It was a tired neighborhood restaurant on a quiet street in the Pacific Beach (PB) area of San Diego, less than two miles from the Pacific Ocean. It seemed like a perfect location. My plan was for a three-story wood-frame building with apartments on the top two floors over ground-floor retail. But one thing's for sure: I had absolutely no intention of fixing up the restaurant. I wasn't stupid, and the last thing I'd ever want to do would be to open an eating establishment.

I ran the numbers and realized that this kind of project could get financing. The owner was retiring and wanted to sell.

Now, many communities across the country have what are called "planning groups," local organizations that decide what they'd like to have built in their neighborhoods. They are advisory only. But often they're quite powerful, so if you come in with a plan they don't like, then you'll have to wait for hell to freeze over before it will ever get approved.

Of course, you might think that certain property rights are inalienable, but you'd be wrong. You might assume that you can build a modern steel-and-glass house in a community of Victorian row homes, but you'd be wrong. You might argue that this is a free society, and you can do what you want with what you own, and you'd once again be wrong. There are rules and there are rights, but in the final analysis, there's the community and there's the local planning group, and you can only do what you can get approved.

I tied up the property and took my proposal to the local community planning group, and they firmly told me that my idea of apartments over retail isn't what they had in mind. What they wanted was for me to keep the restaurant and maybe fix it up a little, but they didn't want to tear it down because they were local folks, and they liked eating there.

Welcome to the fascinating concept of being told what you can do with your property, which you think you control. The community wanted a new restaurant, but they wanted me to build it. I was inclined to tell them that if they wanted a restaurant so badly, then *they* should go and buy the property and then they could all go broke, but don't make *me* do it.

I knew nothing about the restaurant business, and I didn't think I could get financing for one. I knew apartments and retail, and that's what I could get financed. In my mind, the group had some nerve telling me what I should do with my property (or, at least, it was tied up with an option, so I sort of owned it).

And the response was polite, as in, "Would you like another cup of tea," but it was also massively negative, as in "Over our dead bodies." I'm always amazed by how people who have no money in a deal feel that they have both the right and the obligation to tell you, the buyer of the property, exactly what they'd like you to do with it. Your money, but their plan. And to my shock and amazement, the irony of that arrangement never seems to bother the guy who has no money in the deal.

So I went back to the broker to complain and explain that this deal wasn't going to happen. And then the broker said to me, "The restaurant comes with a liquor license in the zip code 92109."

Hit the "Pause" button. Rewind. I knew that there were no new licenses being granted in 92109. This community of Pacific Beach is a young person's neighborhood, and it has more bars per person than any zip code in San Diego County. The local office of the ABC had strong jurisdiction and didn't want an increased proliferation of bars there. If you wanted to open a new establishment that sold alcohol in 92109, sayonara, never going to happen. The San Diego Police Department (vice squad) had closed that door.

This is the entrepreneur's dilemma. It's what you don't know that you don't know that will kill you. But I knew that this liquor license might be more valuable than the entire property, where a new liquor license is impossible to get in any other community in San Diego. The local office of the ABC has strong jurisdiction and does not want an increased proliferation of bars there. This truly is the classic case of "You don't know what you don't know." It seemed that I might have a chance to get my hands on the infamous diamond-in-the-rough without having to go to DeBeers and buy one.

Time to pivot. So I headed home to explain to Steve that after serious consideration and a careful review of the economics, we were going into the restaurant business. I made that decision on the drive home.

I walked in the door, gave Steve a kiss, and explained the plan.

His first instinct was to take me to a psychiatric hospital and have me committed, followed by simply pretending that this too would pass, hum a few bars, and take two aspirin for a bad migraine. But because he loves me and because I can be such a force of nature, he went for Plan B: "Sit down and let's have a calm discussion," knowing that if he didn't, he would never sleep in our bed again. And also knowing that at the end of the day, I was going to prevail, but he wasn't going down without taking a few swings.

Steve said, "Darling, that sounds like a terrific idea. But, sweetheart, just curious, my dearest, have you ever worked in a restaurant? Do you have any relevant experience in how a restaurant really works, honey?"

My answer: "Steve, dearest, I'll hire an experienced chef and manager. How hard can it be?"

And so I decided that I was going into the restaurant business. How to buy the property was the next puzzle. The agreed-upon purchase price was $1.7 million. At that time, the Small Business Administration (SBA) was quite active, and they indicated that they could do the deal. As for the liquor license, it was going to be a transfer, not a purchase, so I didn't need to put money into an escrow. At the close, I would get everything.

The SBA rules are Byzantine, to say the least, and the government small-business loan guarantee program doesn't finance things like liquor licenses. They only lend on the building, on the real estate, and you need to own the building and be the operator. But they wouldn't lend any money on the value of the license, so it was time for some creative accounting. The purchase-price allocation needed to be adjusted. The sale price of the land would be $1.65 million, and the liquor license would be shown with a value of $50,000. The SBA lent me 100 percent of the $1.65 million.

And so, in January 2012, I became the proud owner of a dilapidated dump with a broken kitchen, a stopped-up grease trap, and a leaking roof, which was formerly known as the Lamont Street Grill and would soon be known as The Patio on Lamont.

I had plans. My first problem was how to put a team together to run the place. I interviewed 23 different people to be the chef. Some guys came with attitude; they saw me as a newbie girl, ripe for exploitation, and they saw themselves as next up on the Food Channel, setting the menu and the vision. I didn't need vision; I needed someone who could cook and wouldn't be a prima donna. The restaurant itself had to be dog-friendly and neighborhood-approachable. I finally found my chef, John Medall, an escapee from a big Sheraton hotel kitchen. He had it all: skill, passion, and a ponytail. He was my guy. And he brought along a gang of real talent with experience, so we just made it up as we went along. I called us "The Island of Misfit Toys."

One day while I was sitting in my under-construction restaurant, my phone rang. Out of the blue, it was a guy named Bob Jones from Whittier, California. Jones was buying the Sage Bar and Grill, a restaurant with a liquor license. He'd been referred to me by Bill Adams. In the restaurant industry, Bill was affectionately known as "Wonder Boy" because his knowledge of the arcane rules and circuitous route to getting a liquor license was legendary. The purchase price of the liquor license was $100,000, and he'd "heard" through the grapevine that I understood liquor licenses, so maybe I could lend him the dough so he could complete the transaction.

The road to hell is paved with good intentions, but the other aphorism is: "Don't look a gift horse in the mouth." I went with the second one.

I told him I thought I could put it together for him, and how did 18 percent interest sound? He said it sounded fine. My friend Deborah Patterson and I each put up $50,000, and now I was not only in the restaurant business but also in the liquor-license lending business.

Five months later, Jones got his license, and Deborah and I got back $118,000. This kind of thing could really begin to grow on you. The truth is, I had no intention of going into the financing of liquor licenses. The Jones deal was just a one-off while I was preparing to open my restaurant. It didn't cause too much brain damage, and the return was strong. The size of the deal was modest enough. My focus was on wanting to hear the sound of those martini shakers at the grand opening.

But life has a way of intervening while you're making other plans. Wonder Boy sent me five more license financing deals during the next nine months while I was working on The Patio. They were all in the $100,000 range, and I needed investors to make the loans. Sure enough, just when you need an ace on the river, it shows up. The old guy at the Farms Golf Club, Kim Peterson, had heard about that first deal, and he said he wanted in and that he could finance all of them. And then my friend Lori, across the street from the restaurant, wanted to put in some money, and then two other pals wanted in on the deals.

All in all, we did a total of six legal license deals. They all closed successfully, and although you couldn't really get rich doing this, it was still a solid return and relatively easy money.

But then Kim, the main liquor-license investor, came to me and wanted to do more license deals. He was a wealthy real estate developer, and he thought this 18 percent business was a potential gold mine. To me, it was a distraction.

On November 18, 2012, The Patio on Lamont opened its doors. It was a big deal. The sound of the martini shakers gave me the shivers. I looked across the sea of people at the bartenders and the smiling customers and experienced the love and approval I'd always wanted. And I wanted to do it again.

The classic nightmare for a restaurateur is that either no one comes or everyone comes. In this case, there was a line out the door. Heavy hitters from real estate and politics flooded the place. To get a table, you had to know someone who knew me. I stood at the back for a moment and looked out on the scene. It was incredible. And at that moment, sure, I always knew I wanted to be in the restaurant business.

People were hungry, and the restaurant fed them. But the investors were hungry also, and they were pushing for more license deals. I had to feed the beasts or feed the patrons—or maybe do both. If I wanted to build a restaurant empire, I was going to need a lot more money.

And, oh, I may have neglected to mention one thing: I still needed to raise more money to finish the tenant improvements. About $600,000.

*** ***

CHAPTER 8
Picking the Numbers
Eeny, meeny, miny, moe, pick a number
by its toe.

People often ask, "When did the Ponzi scheme start?" At what moment did I decide to do *illegal* liquor-license loans?

It was a rainy Saturday in early January 2013, around 11:00 p.m. Steve was asleep, and I was sitting at the computer in my upstairs office at my house in Mission Hills overlooking San Diego Bay. Ten years ago, we'd bought it for $1.2 million. It was community property. My three dogs were asleep at my feet. Steve didn't care much for the dogs, but that was part of the deal—the dogs and I were a package.

The Patio on Lamont restaurant had just opened in November. The rain was steady, and I had work to do. Where was I going to get the $600,000 to finish the damn thing? Business was strong (although we were still losing money), but when I asked a few folks about investing in the restaurant, I got crickets. They liked eating there, but nada for an investment of money.

By this time, I'd already successfully funded a half dozen liquor-license loans. The word had spread that I had investors who were interested in doing hard-money loans for these licenses. The community of brokers who worked in this space was small, and they all knew "Wonder Boy" Bill Adams, who was the local king of the liquor-license business. I'd used Bill for the House of Blues and as a facilitator for The Patio on Lamont.

And, of course, there was Kim Peterson, who wanted to do more loans. He liked the return. We were getting 18 percent straight up, not an APR, and if the loan funded in six months, the "return on equity" was closer to 36 percent. I could see why Kim was hot to trot.

It was Bill who had the network of "liquor-license locators," a fancy term for a broker who tries to connect people needing a license with people who are selling a license. You needed to find that match before you went looking for money. The license locators were no different from the brokers in the real estate industry. Buying a house is a once-in-a-lifetime event for most people, which makes the process a bit daunting. The same is true for the average Joe who's opening a bar or restaurant, and the secret code words needed to get it done are the province of the locators. Some of the process resembled a proctology exam.

I had always used Chicago Title for my real estate deals, so it was completely rational to use them for the liquor-license deals, and on their website, they said they did these kinds of deals. Seemed like a no-brainer . . .

The escrow officer on all my deals had always been Joanne Reynolds, and she was famous in the field. She was the queen, and every developer wanted to use her. There was no one better.

It was simple. On that first loan, we put the money into the escrow at Chicago, and Joanne showed the receipt to the local escrow company in Whittier, who filed Form 226 with the ABC to prove that the collateral was in place. The license was approved, and the borrower paid us off, just like it was supposed to happen. Clockwork. By the end of December 2012, my little gang had closed three deals, with three more in the works.

So I got to thinking. Kim Peterson wanted deals; Lori Libs, the chiropractor across from The Patio, wanted deals, so maybe what I needed to do was find some more deals. Kim was all over me, telling me he could do big money, that he had investors who liked this kind of action. His words were: "We need more licenses." He saw liquor-license lending as hard money on steroids. He was like a dog in heat. But you needed to find people who wanted licenses, and people who were selling licenses. It was a matching problem, and frankly, it was a fairly small market.

In California, in 2013, there were only about 100,000 active licenses, in a state with about 35 million people. At any given time, there might just be a few dozen licenses actively being bought and sold in each of the 58 counties. Bottom line: This was beginning to look like needle-and-haystack time. The first few were easy, but at scale, this was going to be a challenge. It was time to check in with Wonder Boy.

Bill told me that he could hook me up with a few locators in Bakersfield, but when I called, they only had two for sale. And a lot of the licenses that were floating around were inactive. Slim pickings. And Kim kept yapping at me about "more licenses." I mean, did he think they grew on trees?

I was facing the classic problem of the two-sided marketplace. I needed to match buyers who needed money and sellers who had licenses.

In 2013, the ten-year Treasury note rate was approximately 1.92 percent. In other words, getting an 18 percent return on your money was pretty awesome, especially if you believed that the loan was safely ensconced with an escrow company like Chicago Title, which itself had a multibillion-dollar parent (Fidelity National Title Insurance); and that the license would only be released when it was funded by the applicant, along with the applicant paying those wonderful fees.

Or as an alternative, the license would be denied, and the loan principal would be returned to the investors. It looked like a no-lose proposition. No wonder Kim was wound up.

***

It was still raining, so I thought I'd take a quick spin around the ABC website. The site didn't list all 100,000 licenses in in the State of California. I couldn't do a global query; that database didn't exist, or if it did, it wasn't accessible. The only way you could look up a specific license was to know either the name of the applicant (the licensee), the location of the establishment (the business address on the application), the business name (for example, Joe's Bar and Grill), or the license number, such as 3803 (this is a real license at 1833 Garnet Avenue in San Diego).

And in 2013, the ABC didn't have very sophisticated software that explained the current status of a license. When you found one, it simply listed it without explaining its history or whether it was in use or inactive. The website was rudimentary, and without putting too fine a point on it, was open to "exploration or exploitation."

I walked out on my deck. It was still raining, but I wanted to feel it. I just stood there getting soaked, thinking about the $600,000 I needed. I was good at math, so I knew that if an average license sold for about $100,000, then six licenses would do the trick.

I'd opened Lamont before it was complete. I didn't want to miss out on the holiday season, and I knew the inspector and yada yada yada, I got the Certificate of Occupancy before all the work was completed, promising him that I'd get it buttoned up in 30 days, and after a couple martinis, what can I tell you, it's America.

The back of the restaurant was closed off with a drop cloth, it needed drywall, and one of the bathrooms lacked a sink and a toilet, I still owed the contractors, so to finish, all in, I needed $1 million. The restaurant had some buzz; and an investor group, headed by Jack McGrory, a big shot, had put up $400,000. I told him that I had "soft-circled" the other $600,000, and not to worry. As a real estate developer, that would be called an optimistic, forward-looking statement. "Soft-circle" means you have verbal commitments.

After all, who would want to invest in a restaurant? The mortality rate in the first year is 60 percent. A restaurant investment masquerades as a tax loss in waiting. But think of the upside: you can always get a table on Saturday night at 7:00 p.m.

I came in out of the rain, put on a dry shirt, gave Stevo a kiss on the head (he was still sound asleep), and went back to perusing the ABC website, hoping to find some applicants.

That evening I couldn't find a single license that was being sold, let alone six. I needed to borrow some money to finish the restaurant, and to do so I needed to offer collateral for the loan. And since no one wanted the collateral of owning a piece of a very hot restaurant, perhaps I could just "create some collateral" that the group would feel good about—namely, six liquor licenses.

This was the first of my "moments." After all, if the investor you want in the deal is buying apple pies, then don't bring him banana cream and try to convince him how good it tastes. Never try to beat the macro. And, of course, it was only a loan, so I figured I could always refinance Lamont and pay it back.

But then I had an interesting idea. What if I "facilitated" both sides of the loan? The investors existed, but what was missing were some licenses and applicants. All I needed was to bundle up a tranche of six licenses, which, admittedly—at least at that moment—weren't really for sale, but by the time they were "approved," I'd be able to pay the money back from the refinance. I viewed it as a short-term bridge loan, what you might call creative financing. And borrowing $600,000 was well within my ability to repay once the restaurant started generating cash flow. It was a win-win.

But you can't just invent a license. It's not like you can simply make up some numbers out of thin air. I would need to find a *real* license number, attached to a *real* restaurant. I mean, the guy owning the restaurant is using the license, and I'm not really selling his license out from under him, so in my mind, it was no harm, no foul. I just needed to virtually "hypothecate" it for a while; it wasn't like he was going to miss it. I just needed to borrow "the license number" for a few months. It wasn't like I was borrowing the actual license; I was merely borrowing the number. See?

It was still raining, but now I felt like I was finally getting somewhere.

Next problem. How exactly was I going to find a license number without knowing the business address or the name of the applicant/owner? But if I could find a real license number, then all the other information would just pop up: applicant, type of license, location, and so on.

I just started punching numbers into the search query box of the ABC website. I became a human random-number generator. And when the three cherries on the slot machine showed up, there would be a real license with a real number with a real owner. I knew the various types of licenses, and because I'd gotten a few of them myself, I knew the basic first numbers that were common for many of them to start with, so I became sort of an Alan Turing, mining for licenses instead of breaking the German code.

It was trial and error. I would go to the license-number page and put in a random set of six digits—let's say four, six, two, five, one, two. Submit. And if there was an actual match, then the data would come up.

As an example, let's say those numbers show that the primary owner of that license is the American Legion in San Diego. It's a Type 51, which is a club, and it's an active license number. It looks like it was transferred on February 2, 2010, from a different license number. The old license number was 57262. And that happens a lot. Sometimes the ABC, for a variety of reasons, will assign you a new license number, or they'll continue with the old license number. However, the page wouldn't tell you whether there were current escrows involved in this license. That turned out to be quite helpful. It made it hard to do due diligence on any given license.

The last thing they listed would be any pending disciplinary actions or operating restrictions.

So there was a hit with the American Legion, San Diego. The ABC site then showed the name of the listed owner. In this case, it was a man named Carl Fredrick DeLuise. He was known as the Commodore, so that's how I could get a name, a business, and an address. And now I had a license that I could put into an "escrow" at Chicago Title.

But as the plan began to take shape, I came upon a new problem. What if an investor knew the restaurant that the license was attached to, and what if he walked in and said to the owner, "Hey, Sam, why are you selling your liquor license? Are you going out of business? What's up?" I knew then that I had to look for locations outside of San Diego. After all, what if you pick a license and one of the investors happens to know the owner at 1833 Garnet, and he wanders in for a drink and asks him why he needs to borrow money to get a liquor license after he was just served a margarita, and it appears he *has* a liquor license. What if he were sleeping with the owner's wife? You can see that this was a potential complication.

The solution was simple. All the licenses would have to be in Northern California, far away from San Diego, so the likelihood of that occurring would be reduced. That *did* make the search a bit more difficult, but it made sense.

So, each evening for the next couple of weeks, after Steve went to bed, I pounded the keyboard looking for numbers. I refined my searching skills and became more selective, looking for licenses that had expired or were pending, but not active. Those would be too dangerous.

I had to find licenses far away enough that the investors weren't going to get in their cars and check out Joe's Bar and Grill in Petaluma. That could prove embarrassing.

It turns out that my guess was correct. No one ever checked the restaurant. Truth is, investors are lazy. After all, why would anyone want to drive to Petaluma in the first place?

The dilemma I faced is that investors wouldn't loan me money for the restaurant—and now I was starting to think about opening others— and additional real estate ventures. But they'd loan money on liquor licenses. As long as I could generate cash flow from my other projects, I could always pay people back on time. They were loans, and I fully intended to repay them in full.

But for now, I only needed to do *one* deal, one simple deal with six licenses, for $600,000. And that is *exactly* what I did.

Sitting at the computer that night, I looked out the window, and through the rain, I could see the future. At least far enough into the future that I could finish the restaurant. And like Scarlett O'Hara, I knew that tomorrow was another day.

And then it stopped raining.

*** ***

CHAPTER 9

Chicago Title

What if the 800-pound gorilla liked money more than bananas?

E very Ponzi scheme needs an inside team and an outside team: someone writing the books, and someone cooking the books. No one can pull off a $400 million scam without some assistance. It doesn't necessarily take a village, but it does take a few willing participants and helpers. One of the key reasons why investors were willing to participate in the liquor-license loan program was because they believed they were sending their money to be held in individual loan escrow accounts at Chicago Title, which was owned by Fidelity National, a public company that generated $8.4 billion in revenue in 2019. And the documents that Chicago generated for the investors showed that the money was right there for safe keeping, which it was.

What they neglected to mention was that the money was in a Master Escrow Account in my name, under my sole control. When I needed money for a deal or to meet payroll at one of my companies, I just asked Chicago to transfer it to me, and they did just that.

The key Chicago Title employees who worked on my liquor-license account were Thomas Schwiebert, VP major accounts (24 years at the company); Adelle (Della) DuCharme, senior commercial escrow officer (22 years); and Betty Elixman, escrow officer, (10 years).

As of this writing, there are eight active lawsuits outstanding against Chicago Title. And also as of this writing, Chicago has paid out more than $100 million in settlements with investors, with ostensibly more to come. But that part of the story is still way down the road.

For now, let's understand how a title company makes money handling these liquor-license escrows: Basically, they charge a base escrow fee of $3,000 for each escrow and $500 for each wire, both ways, in and out. The average investor/escrow generated about $4,500 in fees, and over the seven-year run, there were more than 2,000 escrows. So, you do the math. I figure that Chicago got about $8 million in fees . . . and fees are why people do things.

Multiple attorneys are representing the investors in lawsuits against Chicago Title, and one attorney stands out in particular: Mike Kirby. He reached a settlement with Chicago Title, recovering about $22.6 million for his 48 investors, or approximately 75 cents on the dollar. You may remember that Kirby's firm represented me in my disagreement with Steve Hanson on the House of Blues. I like the guy.

The chief attorney representing Chicago Title against the onslaught of allegations is Steve Strauss, who is "first chair trial lawyer" in the global litigation department of the Cooley Godward law firm. Kirby and Strauss are two of the best. Goliath versus Goliath seems like a fair fight.

In order to give you some insight into the role of Chicago Title, I'm providing some direct material from the lawsuit filed by Mike Kirby on behalf of his group of investors. Please remember that this is what is alleged by the plaintiffs. However, in fairness, there are another half dozen lawsuits in process, and all of them allege approximately the same set of facts.

From the Kirby lawsuit:

> "But what may have started out as a legitimate business proposal very soon became a massive fraudulent Ponzi scheme, which could only exist and continue through the assistance and involvement of Chicago Title and its employees. As described below, it was the national reputation and financial strength of Chicago Title and the promised security of Plaintiffs' loans/investments being safely held by Chicago Title that permitted Champion-Cain to collect more than $200 million in this Ponzi scheme.

> "Lenders/investors were told that Chicago Title was very experienced in the business of handling liquor license escrows, which was confirmed on the public Chicago Title website, and that Chicago Title handled such escrows for Champion-Cain and ANI's business.

> "Lenders/investors were told the money they loaned/invested would never leave the escrow accounts at Chicago Title without the written consent of the lenders/investors or would be flipped into new liquor license escrows, which made sense because Plaintiffs' experiences with escrows were that none of their money deposited into an escrow would be transferred out of an escrow without signed written instructions by them permitting the escrow holder to do so.

> "While Champion-Cain appears to be the original architect of this fraudulent scheme, she received substantial and repeated assistance from Chicago Title's employees to pull off this fraudulent Ponzi scheme and keep it going for several years. She conspired with Chicago Title employees about the need to represent to lenders/investors that the liquor license escrow lending program existed when it in fact did not exist. Chicago Title employees willingly participated

in making false representations to lenders/investors. This fraudulent scheme and conspiracy could not have existed at all, particularly for over 6 years avoiding lender/investor or regulatory detection, except for the ostensible and actual involvement of Chicago Title as the required reputable escrow holder for loans supposedly being made to liquor license applicants. But there were no such liquor license loans or liquor license escrows at Chicago Title, despite Chicago Title's false written and oral representations and confirmations to the contrary."

And the lawsuit goes on for another 434 pages with attachments. But the above represents the basic actions that allegedly supported the idea that the money was being safely held and would not be released without permission.

You know, I *needed* Della and Betty, but I often wondered why they participated. I mean, I gave them a few perks—some trips, a couple of modest checks—but I was in for millions, and they were making their paycheck plus a few thousand in bonuses from Chicago. Of course, Chicago was also making its millions. It's just interesting to understand how people act in their own best self-interest.

I guess in the end, people want to be loved, they want to feel special, and they want to "belong." That's why there is Clubhouse, Instagram, Facebook, Snapchat, YouTube, Tik Tok, Twitter, and probably another handful by the time this book goes to press. I treated these two Chicago ladies like queens in the Court of Gina. I couldn't have done it without them.

Della, Betty, and Tom were all named by Kirby, but there was one additional defendant who was also named:

"Defendant Kim H. Peterson ('Peterson') is an individual residing in San Diego County, California and was previously a practicing attorney in Colorado, where he allegedly had experience with liquor licenses, before moving to

San Diego County. Peterson actively solicited loans or investments for over $150 million in total for the liquor license escrow lending program through his 26 entity Kim Funding, LLC ('Kim Funding'), a professed affiliate of ANI. Peterson and/or his entity, Kim Funding, were substantially compensated for soliciting such lender funds . . . including the right to receive 75% of ANI's profits. From 2012–2019, Peterson initiated or completed over 450 wires to Chicago Title totaling over 280 million dollars."

You know, Kim really was a piece of work. When he first came to me back at The Patio on Lamont and told me he could raise millions of dollars, the original deal he struck was for him to get 80 percent of the profits. I guess greed and guilt must have overcome him later, because after a few years, he offered to change the deal to 75 percent for him. What a sport.

I tell you, I don't think Kim ever focused on the details of the deal. After all, did he really think I was going to do all this work for only 25 percent of the profits? Truth is, after paying the investors their return, and Kim taking some huge fees, there really wasn't much "profit" to split between us anyway. But there was really no reason for me to argue with him about the fees or that 5 percent, when I had access to 100 percent of the money anyway.

In the deal business, you always want to understand who the sucker at the table is. And you know the story—if you can't figure it out, then it's *you*.

Another defendant named in the Kirby litigation was the California Opportunity License Fund, LLC, with Ilan Awerbuch, Merit Financial, and Gina Champion-Cain as the managers. In a public YouTube post, on January 19, 2018, Awerbuch stated:

"Hello, this is Ilan Awerbuch with Merit Financial. I've been asked to say a few more words about the investments that we offer. I run an investment fund called the California Opportunity License Fund, LLC. We're based in San Diego, and we make loans in California. All our loans are bridge loans where the money stays in a licensed escrow, and our borrowers are referred to us by California attorneys who have vetted the borrowers and brought them to us for these bridge loans. It's a complex process, but something I can explain to you reasonably. We have paid eight percent to our investors for the past three years and expect to be able to continue that. Since it's a Reg D registered fund, I have a private placement memorandum, subscription agreement, and an operating agreement that I'm happy to send you. And before that, a two-page overview that will explain what we do, and how we do it. I look forward to hearing from you if you are an accredited investor. And I will tell you that this is a boutique investment, and I will go from there as we have a chance to talk."

When I read this, I called Ilan and told him that I really liked the use of the word *boutique*. It sounded like a restaurant with an unlisted number.

More from the Kirby lawsuit:

"Levin (the named Plaintiff for the case) meets with Elix- man and is shown a list of liquor licenses that Chicago Title was then purportedly processing and Elixman explained that all the money from lenders/investors was deposited into a master escrow account at Chicago Title to fund all of the separate liquor license escrows. Elixman told Levin that the money from lenders/investors never left Chicago Title until close of the license applicants' escrow because the money only moved from the master escrow account to individual ABC applicant escrows."

That was not the truth. This program would never have worked with- out the formation and execution of the one Gina Champion-Cain Master Escrow Agreement. Notwithstanding what people thought or wanted to believe or were told, there were *never* any individual escrow accounts that mirrored each individual license.

More from Kirby:

> "However, in fact, from 2013 through 2019, Chicago Title did not sign or submit to the ABC any completed Form 226, relating to this purported liquor license escrow lending program. It was not until the SEC Action on August 28, 2019, that the investors learned what had transpired, and that the majority of the representations made by both Gina and by Chicago Title were false.

> "For example, when Champion-Cain needed $100,000 on March 21, 2016 to close a transaction, she sent an email to DuCharme saying: *Just to keep you in the loop baby doll . . . I'll just have you transfer over from the handy dandy escrow holding acct...*" [italics added]

Let's take a break here. In retrospect, I would like to have that email back. It was inartful, to say the least. You know the "e" in email doesn't stand for "electronic"; it stands for "evidence." Not my finest hour, by any stretch.

More from Kirby:

> "Chicago Title knew or should have known it was not operating a true escrow account, but rather had created a bank account for Champion-Cain and her business entities and falsely called it an 'escrow.' When, one of the investors wanted to confirm receipt of funds and called Chicago, the request was routed to Gina, who then sent an email to DuCharme: *By the way, he is a total pain in the ass. I'm gonna have grouchy Kim Peterson replace Steve's funds as Kim, as grouchy as he is, is MUCH easier to deal with . . . love that guy! :) I have always promised you I would shelter you from my crazy investors and I will continue to do so. If anyone* [sic] *of*

them bug you as they are too stupid to understand the program, then they are 'FIRED' as an investor!!!! I have plenty of dudes dying to give me money, honey!!! Ahahahahahahahaha. :-D Love you ladies!" [italics added]

This email was painful to see in print in a lawsuit, but I did write it. Arrogant. Embarrassing. Never again. But as a small defense, there was a camaraderie that the team had.

The Chicago ladies and a couple of my own women at ANI—well, we took a certain delight in what we did, just us girls against the world—the world that wouldn't lend us money for legitimate real estate projects, the world that wouldn't invest in my restaurants, the world that wanted me to wear St. John knits, the world that treated smart women with disdain. Sure, women are nice to have in the room, especially if they're pretty, but if it was a really good idea, then let's be sure they share the credit with a man who has a family and looks more like us, rather than a pushy broad with a gorgeous smile, who, if we're not careful, will come in, take over, and eat our lunch—and eat it in front of us at her own restaurant.

We were Thelma and Louise redux. It was joyriding with the top down on a straight road going 50 miles per hour over the limit. It was blast-off, exuberant fun—as long as we didn't wrap it around a pole, James Dean–style.

Complicity in a crime of this magnitude feels dangerous and sexy, dancing to a raging, adrenaline-fueled sing-along: "We are stickin' it to da man." Della and Betty and my assistant, Joelle—we all had roots going back a long way in the male-dominated world we grew up in. We knew about the glass ceiling; we knew about discrimination. But sometimes you just have to say *Fuck it*.

After all, in retrospect, there must have been some element of revenge. Most of the investors were white men making 9 to 16 percent returns on their money, using the efforts of this nice, sexy, charming woman that every damn one of them wanted to fuck. Just wire the money to Chicago and don't even think about it.

I was amazed by how few questions the investors asked, and how little due diligence they did. The average person with $50,000 to invest is going along because he knows a guy who knows a guy who already made the same investment, so what the hell, Sundance, if you can't swim, the fall will probably kill you. But not all the investors were mom-and-pop.

Some of the investors were quite sophisticated.

One of the major investors in the program was Ovation Finance Holdings 2, LLC, out of Texas. They invested $25 million. You would think their due diligence would be rigorous.

More from Kirby:

> "On January 17, 2018, auditor KPMG and its client, Ovation, requested written confirmation that Chicago Title held $25,000,000 of Ovation's funds in escrow for a detailed schedule of liquor license applications, as of December 31, 2017.
>
> "That written request to DuCharme at Chicago Title attached a list of 99 purported liquor license applicants, and the purchase price for each. Chicago Title confirmed on January 18, 2018, in writing the following day, as evidenced by a document signed by DuCharme, that Chicago Title held $25,000,000 in escrow in the name of Ovation in some 99 purported separate liquor license escrows."

I concede that it's not easy to always know when someone is lying, but the truth is, all anybody had to do to check out an actual license was to go to the ABC website. "Purported" is just another way of saying false/phony/nonexistent.

More from Kirby:

> "On April 18, 2018, DuCharme spoke with another lender
> in the liquor license escrow lending program, Banc of
> California, who also wanted to reaffirm that the liquor
> license escrow process at Chicago Title was going well.
> As memorialized by the Banc of California representatives
> who spoke with DuCharme, she assured Banc of California
> that the escrow process at Chicago Title was going well."

Everybody wants to be reaffirmed. It makes you feel good. Banc of California was a Kim Peterson deal, and they'd committed to invest $25 million. But Kim was pushing the bank to up the ante to $30 million. This program was beginning to approach Senator Everett Dirksen country: "Pretty soon, you're talking real money."

The Kirby lawsuit got technical and more legal. They actually wanted to examine the definition of the word *escrow*. Claims were made that escrow numbers were allegedly changed. But in the finale, Kirby called Chicago on the carpet:

> "Instead, Champion-Cain could (and did) withdraw funds
> at will in whatever amounts she desired. Lender/investor
> money was coming into Chicago Title's front door and
> into escrow for the liquor license escrow lending program
> and going out Chicago Title's back door by it permitting
> Champion-Cain and her companies to steal the money."

I take exception to the use of the word *steal*. In my worldview, these were always loans, and it was always my intention to repay them. Frankly, given enough time, that's exactly what would have happened. The plug got pulled, and the curtain came down before the final act was finished.

In any Ponzi scheme, the victims as well as the promoters often do a "look-back" to see if there were any red flags waving gently in the breeze. On May 18, 2019, the wind was blowing 90 miles per hour.

That morning, the SEC served up a few subpoenas—to me, ANI, Kim Peterson, and Chicago Title. Just the facts, ma'am. They wanted to see the documents.

More from Kirby:

> "Even after receipt of the SEC subpoenas, however, Champion-Cain and Peterson continued to solicit millions of dollars from lenders/investors. Likewise, Chicago Title continued to receive millions of dollars from lenders/ investors without ever sounding an alarm. But Champion-Cain, Peterson, and Chicago Title never disclosed the existence of the SEC subpoenas to Plaintiffs or to others."

At this time, I was scrambling to see if I could pull off the IPO by bundling all my businesses together. The program was running on autopilot, and Chicago said nothin' to nobody, nor did Kim.

It was during those four months, from May until August 31, when the ball game was called on account of rain—with the SEC, the FBI, and the U.S. Attorney's Office up by seven runs. Kim alone brought in more than $19 million of new investment money, and it all went into Chicago Title. What were they thinking? That the subpoenas were somehow going to somehow disappear in a cloud of smoke? That the SEC had perhaps made a mistake? It was madness.

I'd created a whirlwind, and it seemed as if there was no way to stop it. At the very end, the SEC asked me why the employees at Chicago Title were willing to go along with the scheme. My answer was that they should ask them directly, but here are some thoughts from the Kirby lawsuit:

> "Tom Schwiebert received numerous benefits or items of value from Champion-Cain throughout the fraudulent scheme, including, but not limited to, cash payments, free food and drinks at restaurants owned by Champion-Cain, free tickets for luxury suites at sporting events, and free

rounds of golf at high-end golf resorts. On or about January 20, 2018, Della DuCharme received a personal check from Champion-Cain for $13,000, with the memo notation 'gift.' Notably, this was just days after DuCharme falsely confirmed to KPMG that Chicago Title held $25 million in escrow for specific liquor license applications as of December 31, 2017.

"Betty Elixman got a check for $5,000, with the memo notation 'gift.'"

In retrospect, you have to wonder: so for this, the three of you would be willing to lose your jobs and reputations?

The number of times the red flags waved were too numerous to count. I think toward the end, I was just waiting to get caught. The program had a life of its own, and by that time, I was just along for the ride on a runaway train.

During the program, various lawyers sent due-diligence teams to Chicago and to the bundlers to review and explore the legalities of the platform before they sent in their money. On balance, everyone gave it a thumbs-up. It was the classic case of hiding in plain sight.

From a lawyer's letter to his client: "During the seven years of the Platform with thousands of escrows successfully closed and fees paid to the Platform, not one complaint has been received from the ABC or an Applicant as to the Platform's processes or fees."

Not one. What are the odds that not one complaint would come up, and that heads would come up 100 percent of the time? Ask yourself.

*** ***

CHAPTER 10

The Bundlers

I know a guy who knows a guy.

Part 1

O kay, so I figured out how to generate liquor-license loan numbers, and admittedly, not all of them were legitimate. Actually, very few of them, but no one knew or even did basic due diligence.

I'd arranged the Master Escrow Account at Chicago Title, which essentially acted as a personal piggy bank. Just a note here: they don't do Master Escrow Accounts any longer. I wonder why.

So all I needed now was the money to grow my business empire. And that leads us to that not-so-famous movie, *Meet the Bundlers*. Besides random individual investors, the majority of the money raised came from seven major promoters. They had clients who wanted higher-than-normal returns, and like all promoters, they didn't do this for their health, or for the health of their clients; they did it for the fees. And they charged their clients fees on the one side, and they charged me fees on the other. Both ways, nice work if you can get it.

The amount of help and the ease in getting money still surprises me. Several of the bundlers were fighting with each other over whom I loved the most: Was one guy's deal better than another? Who should get priority to lend on which license groups? How much were the fees? You know how they say everything is high school redux? Well, they're right. Grown men wanting to be loved and get richer; and yes, I did make all of them a little crazy at times, but hey, why not? Just like in high school.

So what was in it for the bundlers? Herewith, a short course in high finance:

Bundlers are promoters, salespersons. They're providing access to deals or houses or vacations or opportunities that the common man or woman does not have awareness of, or easy access to. A deal person can show you stocks, bonds, derivatives, straddles, options, and assorted esoteric, but not necessarily bad or inappropriate opportunities; they're simply things you didn't know about because you go to work each day at a company making widgets, and bull-sperm futures aren't on your radar. At the end of the day, you need to know someone who knows someone you need to know.

This is how the program worked. A bundler would solicit investors and would promise them a rate of return of between 9 and 11 percent per annum. The supposed applicant for the license agrees to pay 18 percent straight up, not per annum. So let's assume that this particular tranche of loans is exactly $1 million, and let's suppose that it was "out" for exactly one year. In that case, the payment would be $1,180.000. The 9 percent investor would get $90,000, and the bundler would get $90,000 in "profit," of which I was supposed to get some amount between 20 and 50 percent.

But I never took any profit, or any of my supposed share. And none of them ever wondered why I was "working for free."

In addition, many of the bundlers also got paid an additional "fee" of 5 percent for raising the money. Now, you might ask: Where did the money for that fee come from? There doesn't seem to be enough money in the deal to go around for everyone to get all their fees.

It always amazed me that these financial geniuses, wealth managers, promoters, and big-shot deal guys never did enough math to understand that there was no way this could work. There was never enough juice in the lemon. But like the lawyer said, no one ever complained.

Now we can't leave well enough alone, so let's turbocharge the deal for the bundlers. If that same $1 million loan "pays off" in six months, the investors only get $45,000, because their money was out for only six months at 9 percent, but the bundlers got the full $180,000 (18 percent x $1 million); and so after paying their investors $45,000, they netted $135,000 for the six months.

If you start to do that math on about $400 million over seven years, you can see that bundling was a hell of a business. The thing that made me crazy was that of the approximately 280 people who invested, I personally only knew about 55. Literally, money was wired to Chicago Title from a couple hundred people that I'd never met or talked to. Money just showed up, and Della and Betty would put it in the escrow account along with a list of licenses, and that was it.

The deal was being sold as bulletproof, can't lose. Chicago Title was a gold-plated safe place.

There was this element of exclusivity, the infamous FOMO (fear of missing out), take my money, please, before there's no room.

When someone shows you a deal you didn't know about, it enhances that person's standing because it demonstrates a level of business acumen that you don't have. The fact that you may or may not understand the deal is irrelevant. If Smith is in, then I am too.

Moneylenders and dealmakers in the temple represent an old and practiced profession that started about the 5th century BCE, when coins were first introduced. I suspect that Adam was probably borrowing against the first crop of apples, hedging the commodity market in Jerusalem in order to buy Eve something nice from the garden for her birthday. Buying and selling in the marketplace was as natural as breathing. Lending was a close second. And we were making loans. Lots of them.

Between 2012 and 2019, about $380 million flowed in and out of Chicago Title. A spreadsheet from May 2019 right before the subpoena arrived showed that the investors thought they had $132,895,000 at Chicago Title. In reality, there was about $26 million. Over the seven years, the majority of the bundlers took out all their fees, early investors received all their original investments back, plus interest payments (they're referred to as "net winners"), but many of the investors never took their interest payments out and never got whole, because they wanted more action. So they simply rolled their money back into the next tranche of licenses. As for me, I "borrowed" about $60 million to invest in my businesses: restaurants, retail, and real estate.

Each bundler had a different deal with me.

For example, The Kim Peterson Fund LLC, which facilitated more than $140 million in investment capital into the program, split with me 80–20 initially, and later, in a moment of either panic or gratitude, increased it to 75–25, still in Kim's favor.

Now why would anyone want to be a bundler? After all, there might be some legal liability just in case things didn't work out as planned, but if you assessed that risk as not likely (Google *black swans* and call me back), then the truth is that it was really good work if you could get it.

In order to understand why a bundler bundles, let's look at the cohort of licenses for October 6, 2017. There were 30 licenses in that grouping, and the total loan commitment was identified to be $5,950,000. These were not real licenses for sale, and the prices being asked for those licenses were totally made up. But, as Mark Twain famously said, "Never let the truth get in the way of a good story."

I arranged for these 30 licenses to all have different "starting dates," meaning different dates for the beginning of the escrow agreements. In that way, I could accurately calculate the number of days the money was out and the duration for which interest would be earned. The starting dates for this cohort ranged from November 17, 2017, to December 1, 2017. After all, it would look suspicious if all the licenses started on the same day.

Then, after a period of time, the loans on these licenses would "close," meaning the fake borrower who'd applied for the fake license would get his fake approval from the ABC licensing department, and the fake licensee would then repay the loan that had never been funded, as well as the interest due for having had the loan in an escrow that didn't exist.

The closings were arbitrary and were dictated by when I would have enough new money to close the previous tranche.

These 30 licenses all closed at various times ranging from 143 days to 616 days. Let's examine license #524899 in the amount of $150,000. One investor had invested in that license, and that license "closed" in 143 days. The promoter who arranged that loan was paid a fee of 22.5 percent of the principal invested, or $33,750. That was the interest/fee earned by the promoter on that loan. From that amount, the promoter/bundler had to pay his investor back the interest earned while the investor money was out. For simplicity, we'll ignore the principal repayment, since that was dollar for dollar and no fee was earned, and principal was only repaid if the investor wanted it back.

If the promoter had promised his investor an 8 percent return, that would have amounted to $4,701. This math concept is important, and it's a major reason why people bundle. The investor was paid on an annual percentage interest rate, commonly known as APR. Home mortgages, for example, are required by law to tell the investor that calculation. The key word here is *annual*. Certain individuals/organizations such as loan sharks and the Mafia do not use the word *annual* in their calculations.

So our investor gets 8 percent times $150,000 for the length of 143 days, and that works out to about $4,701, give or take a few days one way or the other. But the promoter was paid $33,750 for that license. He takes the $33,750 and pays his investor $4,701, and he nets approximately $29,000 on that one license. The bundler gets a fixed return, regardless of the length of time the license was open.

On that particular tranche of October 6, 2017, the total invested was $5,950,000. Let's assume that the "investors" in that tranche were paid 8 percent per annum. The various license terms were from 143 to 616 days, but the average length in that tranche of 30 licenses for money to be out was approximately 450 days. And if there was only one promoter who had bundled all that money, and if the rate of return to the investor was 8 percent, the "profit, the interest earned" by the investor, was approximately 8 percent times $6 million for an average term of 15 months, and thus the ballpark amount earned by the investors was $600,000 (calculated as $6 million x 8%/12 = monthly, then x 15 months).

Are you perhaps curious as to how much money was paid to the promoter?

The answer is: $1,611,500. That was the *gross* promoter share, but now he has to pay out the $600,000. After all, the investors are entitled to get their agreed-upon deal, and then since it worked out so well, many of them will, of course, roll it over into a new license so they can make some more money—on paper.

Give or take a few nickels, the net to the promoter on those 30 licenses was $1,011,500. More than 3,000 licenses went in and out over seven years, some being sold multiple times. You do the math. The fees alone were approaching more than $75 million. That was not *my* money, that was *bundler* money.

There were some spins, some twists, and some nuances, but at the end of the day, there was a lot of money sloshing around disconnected from the investors themselves. It was like making sausage: as long as the investors got their ball-game hot dogs with mustard and relish, why go to the packing plant and make yourself ill?

Some of the aggregators just called up their friends, and they sent money in. But some of the more sophisticated bundlers produced full private placement memorandums (PPMs). In that way, they could raise much larger pools of money. These were completely detailed with full legal explanations, along with the requirement that to invest you needed to be an "accredited investor" (that is a term of art that describes certain net-worth statements, and the intent behind that classification is to prevent investment novices from getting involved—the assumption is that if you're accredited, you're sophisticated about investing).

Most of the investors, whether from the individual promoters or from the PPM bundlers—more than 250 of them—were white and rich; sophisticated; owned homes and other real estate; and had stock and IRA accounts. Most were men and women in the 1 percent class, and their investment decision making seemed mostly to rely on the fact that someone else they knew had already done it. You might say it was the blind leading the nearsighted. And no one put on their reading glasses.

Kim Peterson was the keystone investor, and although not everyone knew him, at least they all knew someone in the deal who knew him. It was the classic less than three degrees of separation. And by the same token, that's how I ended up meeting the other bundlers.

An early investor in the original legal liquor-license loans, whom I mentioned earlier, was Dr. Lori Libs, a chiropractor with an office across the street from The Patio on Lamont restaurant. She'd made a little money on those deals, she liked wine, and we became friends. And she was one of the original investors, along with Kim, in the famous "six" licenses that I did to finance the completion of the restaurant.

While that was playing out, I asked her if she wanted to invest in my vacation-rental business (I'd bought a few of those in Pacific Beach and wanted to buy more). She was mildly interested, but she introduced me to her friend, Ilan Awerbuch, who did hard-money loans and was a major player in the space.

I went to see him, but he had no interest in vacation rentals. However, over time, we started socializing. He liked to play the guitar, was a good singer, and held fun parties. We became friends (this is what passes for due diligence), and he wanted to get in on the license loan program.

Ilan's method for raising money was to create a formal PPM called the California Opportunity License Fund, LLC. I was his "silent" partner. Ilan was a master of marketing. Below is an excerpt from the PPM offering document, which explains how his program worked:

CALIFORNIA OPPORTUNITY LICENSE FUND, LLC

Every location that sells alcohol in any form in California needs to have a license issued by the state regulatory authority, the CAABC (California Alcoholic Beverage Control). From gas stations, liquor stores and wineries, to restaurants and micro-breweries, a buyer of one of these businesses must be approved by the ABC. Prior to the ABC beginning its thorough review of that license applicant, there must an escrow established to transfer/ buy the license, and the applicant/buyer must deposit the entire purchase price of the license into that escrow.

The value of an individual liquor license depends on the location and its profit potential; they range from $25,000 on the very low end (a gas station selling beer) to as much as $1,000,000 for an ultra-high end, highly profitable location (beach-front resort), with conditional use features (staying open until 2 AM, allowing live music, etc.).

California liquor licenses are generally transferrable (can be resold), highly regulated, and in short supply in some areas that are under a moratorium. Again, the prospective buyer must place ALL OF THE FUNDS TO PURCHASE THE LICENSE in an escrow acceptable to the CA ABC. This is even the case when an ownership entity/partnership is undergoing any change in its ownership structure. An established business or large corporation would probably have these funds available, but an individual buyer/small group that is counting on a Bank SBA type loan, crowd-funding, or other loan for their business, may not have an easily available source of these funds to place into escrow for 6-10 months.

This is when the CA Opportunity License Fund is available to step in and provide those funds into the escrow. The escrow company being used in these transactions is a very large, well-known, nationwide Title and Escrow provider, and the funds are kept in the individual license escrow until that application has been approved by the CA, ABC. The license applicant/prospective buyer doesn't get to use or have access to the funds. We are placing these funds into escrow, only after the applicant's file has been prepared and vetted by attorneys who work in the area.

After approval by the ABC, the license buyer/applicant or their Bank or SBA replaces our funds on deposit with their own funds, repaying our loan plus the fee earned by our Fund, typically 15%. It is currently taking the CA ABC 8-10 months to complete their approval process, although some have been approved in as little as 4 months and in some rare instances it has taken the ABC upwards of 12–14 months to complete their approval process.

The CA Opportunity License Fund, LLC is co-managed by American National Investments, Inc. (owned by Gina Champion-Cain) and Merit Financial, Inc. (owned by Ilan Awerbuch). The Fund holds a CFL (California Finance Lenders License) issued by the California Department of Business Oversight. CA Opportunity License Fund, LLC conducts an extensive licensing process, including a surety bond. The Fund also operates in accordance with U.S. Reg. D. The two managers have been operating the ANI License Fund I as a Division of ANI, Inc., from August 2014 till the present, taking in their first investment funds in August 2014.

Since that time, the fund has paid out nine consecutive quarterly installments since the first quarter of 2015. Because we are charging the applicants a flat fee for the use of our funds, the faster the ABC approves licenses, the higher the potential return we can earn.

In addition to the ANI License Fund I, several individuals have been lending on liquor license escrows on a personal basis for the past 5 years, so there is a solid track record of these investments performing and generating strong returns. The Fund continues to experience funding requests into escrow of $3–$5 million per month.

If you are interested in reviewing the Fund's Documents (Private Placement Memorandum, Subscription, and Operating Agreements) please contact Ilan Awerbuch or Joelle Hanson and let us know if you would like to receive them. Of course, we encourage and expect you to review the Documents with your significant other, and your trusted financial and legal advisors.

Sincerely,

Ilan Awerbuch,
President

Merit Financial, Inc.

iawerbuch@meritfi.com

Gina
Champion-Cain, President

American National
Investments, Inc.

joelle@americannational
investments.com

In addition to the PPM guys, there were also some major banks and hedge funds, like Ovation Finance, CalPrivate Bank, and Banc of California. The program began to have a life of its own, and from time to time, I hoped it might just stop. It was a runaway train, and I knew there was never going to be a track long enough.

I never really hid the baseball. It amazed me that no one wanted to look. But the failure to look was not unique to this group. The truth is that most of us are afraid to look. Sure, maybe at 15 miles an hour we peer over at the three-car crash, with the fire trucks and the Jaws of Life and women crying and screaming by the side of the road, but then in about ten more seconds, we're back in our own lane, heading to wherever we're going next, glad it wasn't us and assuming the check will clear like always. Greed is a powerful emotion.

One of the other bundlers was Joe Cohen, who ran ABC Funding Strategies, LLC, another formal PPM to solicit investors for the program. Joe is charming and deeply self-aware. Toward the end of the program, he shared a conversation with one of my friends. He told him that he thought part of the problem with any Ponzi scheme is that everybody's greedy—not just the promoters, not just the aggregators, not just the investors, but everybody gets caught up in getting an outsized return. He said, "You know, everybody is making good money."

He told him that it felt like a virus, with plenty of willing hosts who want to tell you how much money they're making. Everyone gets infected with FOMO. Joe was angry with me, sure, but he also seemed to have his own self-awareness, merged with some self-recrimination.

It was hard for him to understand. After all, at one point, five or six different investor groups had gone and done due diligence on Chicago Title and the program. One group from Texas even sent in a cohort from KPMG to do a fine-tooth-comb analysis. Everyone always came back with a clean bill of health. You might ask: How could that be? You know, someone should ask them.

Bottom line: I think our default behavior tilts toward trust. Looking back, you can always find little red flags, but in the moment, they don't seem suspicious, and you just don't see them.

I hope Joe can find forgiveness in his heart for himself, and maybe along the way, at some point, for me as well.

The basic model was to solicit an investment and then have it wired directly to Chicago Title. My little company, ANI, never received any money from investors. I never knew for sure, but I suspect that the fine points regarding their fees were disclosed somewhere, probably in four-point Bodoni disappearing italics, but the truth is, that wasn't my problem. I had to keep the magic ball spinning.

Most of the bundlers were professionals in the business of raising money for investment opportunities. I was simply one among many. No different from your pal at UBS or Morgan Stanley who recommends the XYZ hedge fund or a municipal bond (might be a different risk tolerance there); and gets paid for his insight, guidance, leadership, and financial acumen. Raising money and pooling resources for innovation or financial return is an American pastime.

But the truth is, nobody does nothing for nothing.

***

The reason you use an adviser is to give you access to deals you wouldn't normally see (or might not understand); otherwise, you'd be the promoter. I confess that at times I felt like a Queen Bee in a game of drones. I really liked the attention and being loved. I wanted to keep my drones happy. It's probably my fatal flaw.

One of my favorite bundlers was Horacio Valeiras. He was always complimentary to me, as he admired the detail and rigor we provided for his investors. His 1099s were always on time, and the spreadsheets were complete. He was another guy who gave great parties, and he flew his own jet. He was Argentinian by birth, very successful, and had worked at Nicholas-Applegate, a very successful investment firm. He was worldly, had lived in London, and now had his office in La Jolla. He was the real deal. Kim had known him for a few years, and when you know about something good, it's human nature to want to share it. And so it was that Kim introduced me to Horacio, and we clicked instantly. He became an immediate investor, and I really liked him.

Horacio was known for the elegant entertainment he provided. He threw a large Christmas party every year in his office, with wonderful food and expensive wine. And he became more than mildly engaged with the program. Horacio ran the HAV Global Macro Fund, which invested approximately $18.5 million into the liquor-license program between 2015 and 2017. He also had a couple of smaller investment vehicles to round out his stable, and they threw in another $4 million. All in, let's call it about $22 million, give or take a few dollars. I admired Horacio, but I was also afraid of him. His due diligence was rigorous, and I've always been surprised that he didn't figure it out.

And for some of the investors, I always offered a few perks: getting into the restaurants, the private box at Petco Park for Padres games, and more. Economically not very significant, but people like to feel special. There's nothing like having a reserved parking space near the front door, walking past the gatekeepers, waving your pass, with lots of nods and greetings as you make your way up to the club-level suite, where you're greeted by two lovely ladies who tell you that if you need anything, you don't have to holler—just turn around and they'll be standing at the back of the suite waiting to address your every desire. Petco was the equivalent of a backstage pass to a Bruce Springsteen concert.

Me, personally, I almost never went to a game. I didn't know the investors, and frankly I didn't want to. I had an empire to build.

Part 2

The program was rolling along. I was building my restaurant and retail expansion, and I was working on creating the liquor-license tranches a few times per month. Same place, upstairs office in my home, while Steve was asleep.

The day-to-day activities were run by my two assistants, Joelle Hanson and Rachel Bond. They managed the in and out of money to the various companies I was running, while also dealing with Della and the team at Chicago Title. I don't want to sound arrogant, but it was a well-oiled operation.

But there was one investor who would only deal with me personally. In the SEC complaint, he's known as "Investor #1," the biggest dog in the kennel, Mr. Kim Peterson. You may remember that it was Kim who came to me way back at the start of The Patio restaurant and told me that he could raise millions and he wanted licenses. And sure enough, during the seven-year run, Kim raised more than $130 million.

Kim's a handsome 72-year-old lawyer from Del Mar, a premier beach community known for the Del Mar Racetrack, founded and frequented by Hollywood royalty including Bing Crosby, Lucille Ball, and Jimmy Durante. He's been a real estate developer and a "deal guy" for the last 30 years. He's served on the board of the private Bishop's School in La Jolla, and over the years he's cultivated a "larger-than-life" personality. And how did I meet him? At the Farms Golf Club, where else? I think he liked my backswing.

He has two major passions: skiing and airplanes. He's a real double-black-diamond skier, and as for airplanes, he started with propellers and eventually, when his fortunes increased, he got a small jet. But he never got his own pilot's license. However, his fascination with, and desire to own, airplanes is a recurring theme for him. A plane is an excellent way to demonstrate power and influence, and those two things are quite helpful to have if you're out and about raising money. Kim talked a lot about his plane. But we all know the story—there's always a bigger jet on the tarmac, and of course, that jet belonged to Horacio, and these two guys definitely had penis issues with the jets.

Horacio teased Kim mercilessly about his "small" jet. And the truth is, Horacio not only had a bigger jet, he also had a pilot's license and flew his own plane. They both raised money for me, and they competed for the better deal. Each wanted exclusivity, and I wouldn't give it to either of them.

Kim really liked his plane, and he often invited me to fly with him. One of the most powerful phrases in dealmaking is: "I'll send my plane to pick you up." There's a famous quote attributed to a Hollywood studio executive, who, after ceremoniously stepping down from his black tower glass office on the 87th floor (after he got severance and an office and a secretary and a parking spot), says, "What I will miss most is the corporate jet."

Kim had been pestering me for weeks to go up to Napa and have lunch with him. He'd just funded another $1.2 million into Chicago Title, he was counting his chickens as they hatched, and he wanted to show off to me, so I agreed to meet him at Montgomery Field (an airfield for private planes in San Diego), and we jetted off to Napa.

Well, not exactly *jetted*. Kim's plane was a King Air 300. I mean, it had good speed and it was pleasant, but I'd been in Horacio's Citation Sovereign. That's a *real* jet. But I tell you, this whole plane thing between the two of them seemed stupid. I mean, who the fuck cares as long as it takes off and lands in one piece?

But Horacio had a toilet, and with Kim, I needed to pee before takeoff. And hang on, no beer until we landed.

At any rate, I agreed to the lunch, and after all, I liked making people happy, and since I wanted to keep Kim happy, off I went into the plane. Kim isn't a pilot, so there was a real guy who flies the plane sitting in the cockpit. I asked Kim, "You think maybe two pilots would be safer?" Kim's response was, "Don't worry, no problem, this guy's an expert." My concern, frankly, was not whether he was an expert, it was more like, what the hell were we going to do when the guy has a heart attack, slumps over the stick, we're sitting in the back seat, the plane goes into a nosedive, and I turn to Kim and say, "Okay, hotshot, what do we do now with the expert?"

The pilot did *not* have a heart attack, but you can't fault me for thinking ahead.

It was a gorgeous day, like almost all days in San Diego, and in fairness to the guy in the front seat, the takeoff was perfect, and an hour and 37 minutes later, we landed at Napa County Airport.

During the flight, I had to listen to a technical discussion of turbo-chargers and radar. Kim loves this stuff. You'd think he'd get his own pilot's license, but maybe he knows his limitations. His attention span is modest, so I think he prefers putting his life in someone else's hands rather than his own.

After all, he was putting his financial life in *my* hands, and so far as he knew, he was doing great, making money hand over fist. An airplane is like a yacht; if you have to ask how much the gasoline costs, you can't afford the boat.

In Napa, we went to La Toque, a one-star Michelin restaurant. I had the halibut; Kim had the duck breast. The truth is, I'm just a regular girl, and a good taco at El Indio suits me just fine.

"When can we get more licenses?" seemed to be Kim's main thrust over lunch. I could have told him, "When I get time to go back to the computer and find some," but I didn't say that. I was more polite.

I told him, "Kim, the licenses come up all the time. Just be a little patient."

"I have lots of money waiting for licenses," he said. On that point, I could not disagree. Kim had raised more than $40 million for the program at that point. Ultimately, he would raise over $100 million.

"That's great," I said. "You are numero uno for the licenses. You get to see the best stuff first." This was the same thing I told Horacio. At times, I sounded like an antique dealer or a drug pusher. The best stuff first. Kim likes being first.

Dessert was Jivara ganache with toasted marshmallow cream. How could a girl keep her figure eating like this?

Uber to the airport, and home we go. This time I got to sit in front. I liked looking at all the instruments, which gave me a respite from Kim's lecture on horsepower, adverse yaw, and drag ratio.

Kim remarked, "This was a wonderful afternoon. I love when we can spend quiet time together and not worry about liquor licenses."

"Yes, it is a great relationship," I replied. As long as I keep paying you a 15 percent return and fees. But I didn't add that.

We climbed to 12,000 feet. The sun was shining above the clouds, and for a moment, I was relaxed. The pilot was not Tom Cruise, but he was young and handsome. I knew he was flying Kim so that he could get enough hours to move up to a commercial-pilot rating. My real estate deals were beginning to come together. I was going to expand the coffee stand I'd started and add a whole bean-roasting program. I could sell bean bags retail and do contract grinding for other growers. The sky was blue, and the girls at Chicago seemed content. I drifted off for just a moment. Not much peace in my world, but this was just a moment when there was.

And then there was a speed bump.

Kim said, "You know, Gina, when we land, I'll total up the gas bill, and we can split it."

"Huh?"

"It's not a big deal, but I think we should share the cost of the gas."

And that's when I grabbed the stick and pulled it straight back. The airplane nose went straight up.

Kim screamed, "What the fuck are you doing?!"

The pilot was stunned, and the plane went into a steep climb. I hung on for four more seconds, and the stall warning horn began to scream. Another three seconds, and I let go, and the pilot wrested back the control, pushed the nose down, and once again, we averted sudden death.

Look, I knew a little about planes. We weren't going to crash. I'd been in other planes with other rich clients. I just wanted to make a small but important point to Kim.

"I am *not* splitting the gas bill with you," I told him firmly.

After all, the guy was making millions in fees—gimme a break. You know, I never asked Kim this one question, and maybe I will at some later time: "Kim, you were already rich when you started with me. Just tell me, how much is enough?"

***

Kim and Horacio were at loggerheads with each other a lot of the time. There were only so many licenses, each wanted to pick first, and each wanted their own deal with respect to the fees. And when each of them found out what the other's deal was, well, it was the famous phrase, "This airplane isn't big enough for the two of us."

Their conflict became disruptive and annoying to me, and finally, before things bubbled completely out of control, I suggested they have a "sit-down."

It's true that Horacio had the deeper pockets, the bigger jet, and he'd been the one to give Kim a loan early on in his career, but like the Bob Dylan song, "I was with Big Jim, but I was leanin' to the Jack of Hearts."

Kim wanted to go bigger, and he wanted to take Horacio out. He wanted the whole enchilada for himself. It was Kim who got the lawyer letter that said there was never a complaint from an applicant. But Kim never thought to ask why there was never a complaint. Well, there were no complaints because none of the licenses were ever denied or turned down—because *I* controlled the licenses. Be careful what you wish for; you may get it.

If you think about it, there were multiple opportunities to question the program. You didn't have to be a forensic PhD with knowledge of algorithms or an alcohol-license expert. All you had to do was ask yourself how come none of the licenses ever failed to fund. There was never a statement that said, "Harry's Bar and Grill in Ferndale, California, was denied his license because he was a twice-convicted felon, using a fake name and ID in his application, and we, the ABC caught that anomaly and denied him the license."

Life is filled with ironies. Before coming to San Diego, Kim was an attorney at a law firm in Colorado. His specialty was criminal defense, but the firm itself also specialized in ABC liquor-license representation. I'm not sure *how* exactly, but Kim had lost the tip of his middle finger. It was like a stub. And he had this singularly annoying characteristic of constantly shoving that stub in my face when he was emphatically making a point. I always felt as if I were on the witness stand with that stub poking at me.

Kim was a difficult guy to deal with, so I worked hard to keep him away from the Chicago Title girls. First, I thought he would piss them off; and second, he might ask too many questions—some of which I've always suspected he already knew the answers to.

I told him, "You would kill those girls, Kim. Just let them do their work." I felt that if he started to grill them, they might just walk away from the program. When I froze him out from them, he would get outraged, shove that stub into my face, and tell me that he wasn't a difficult guy—he was smart and knew how to talk to people. That's always what smart, difficult people think.

Kim liked to talk up his successes. He was a raconteur and could tell a good story about his financial and business acumen. He would have you believe he bought Tesla at three. But like most of us, he had a very casual memory with respect to his losses.

So I put my foot down and demanded the summit. Kim had come to me that morning to tell me that his plan was simple. He was going to buy Horacio out—take him out of all the deals, pay him off, and that would be the end of the matter.

Envy and jealousy are said to be the motivation behind Cain murdering his brother, Abel; his solution was to hit him with a stone. That was how they handled things back in the first century BCE, but when Kim and Horacio agreed to meet, they left their stones unturned in the lobby. There was no way *I* was attending that meeting.

I don't know what was said, but later that evening Kim gave me the tale of the tape: "I told Horacio that he was getting too rich and that I wanted to renegotiate our deal."

Horacio had been the early financing lender to Kim Funding, LLC. Kim would borrow from Horacio and then send the money to Chicago Title to invest in the program, and Horacio would receive a fee for the money, paying him around 13 percent for much of his money. Well, it doesn't take a PhD in quantum mechanics, let alone arithmetic, to understand that if the juice in the deal averages 16 to 18 percent, then after the payout to HAV, there wasn't much left for Kim, let alone droplets for Gina. Horacio was Kim's expensive seed money, and he wanted to get the monkey off his back, so to speak.

Kim told me that he no longer needed Horacio, and that he could get all the way home on his own. His money was just too damn expensive.

But sometimes it's easy to forget how you got where you are. You get confused and begin to think you did it on your own. Kim had brought the program to Horacio very early on because Horacio had a lot of money, knew a lot of money, and when Kim wanted to "go big," he'd need some significant firepower. And the big dog gets to eat what he kills—and sometimes take a bite from the other dog's meal as well. And then the smaller dog barks and wants to reset the table with new silverware.

But Horacio believed that because he'd been early to the party, his deal was appropriate. After Kim explained that he'd be buying out Horacio, Horacio stood up, circled in front of his desk, put his nose in Kim's face, and said that if there was any buying out, it would be *him* buying out Kim. Horacio said he could raise $500 million, and size matters, and that Kim would be a dead man walking. You can pick up your check on the way out.

The way Kim told it, there was a standoff. Whoever blinked first was done. The bell rang for the next round, and it looked like it was headed for a split decision, and then there was one of those newspaper moments where the reporter says, "Shots were fired. The discussion continued." I wish I'd been there, but in the end, Horacio agreed to the deal, Kim borrowed $25 million from Banc of California to take him out, and as we now all know, it was Horacio who dodged the bullet.

And frankly, so did I.

I never wanted Horacio as the primary. He was shrewd, and he would have figured the ins and outs of the program, and then he would have taken control and gone and made nice with Bill Adams (the Wonder Boy liquor lawyer), and then he would have gotten cozy with the Chicago Title gals, and then he would have eventually kicked me to the curb, and my plans would have been aborted before they could be realized. I did not want to tussle with Horacio. Kim, I could manage.

Several years later, when the music stopped, the SEC complaint would refer to Peterson as "Investor #1," which clearly made him "king of the hill, top of the heap." No mention of you, Horacio—this was your "missing the flight" moment. If Kim wanted to take your seat on the plane, the one with no landing gear, well, count your lucky stars. You just won the "Warren Buffett, You Can Never Go Broke Taking a Profit" award.

And then the craziest thing of all happened: Horacio got "the itch." He wanted back in. It's the same old story, a fight for love and glory—and greed. You see other people getting rich, and then the gnawing starts, the phone isn't ringing like it used to, and after all, this liquor-license lending program is a no-brainer. So you think, well, WTF, I need to get back in the game, and then in a moment of madness, even though you got all your money back once, you go back into the program in late 2018, lending money to Kim again (albeit at a lower rate). You get divorced once, and then you find you can't live without her, and you remarry the same woman.

And so we come to spring 2021, the program is over, broken glass is everywhere, and Horacio and Kim are both in litigation, along with several hundred others, all wanting to get their money back.

Dude, you got it back once. What were you thinking?

Part 3

To this day, I continue to be amazed by how much money the promoters, enablers, and bundlers were able to raise. Maybe they were using the Nigerian-prince marketing model. The liquor-license loan program seemed to have a life of its own, and by the end of the run, I'd personally known no more than 50 or 60 investors. The vast majority simply seemed to show up.

They would get a call, then get sent some material they didn't read, then ask who else was in the deal, and then flip to the signature page, sign it, initiate a wire transfer, and head out to lunch at the club, or whatever. It was crazy.

There was a bit of FOMO going on all the time. You can imagine the call to an investor: "There are only so many licenses in each tranche, Harry, and once that tranche is committed and filled, you'll have to wait for the next one, and I don't know when that will be coming around, and I don't want you to miss out on this golden opportunity . . . and by the way, how are the kids?"

You know, I've been doing deals for a long time, and when I get a call for a deal that's a slam dunk, a "You can't pass this one up" kind of deal, I ask myself the following question: *How is it that I'm so special that he called me?* This is a critical moment when considering an investment decision. If this is a slam dunk, a can't miss, how did I get so lucky? Then unless you're the promoter's brother-in-law who owes you thousands of dollars, or you have a picture of him with a donkey; and unless there's some compelling, overarching, absolutely clear reason that you're getting a shot at this first, then this is worth repeating: *It's because you're not getting it first.* And the reason I know this is because you're *never* first.

You are the nth call he's made, hoping to fill out the deal and get his fees. People do not normally act altruistically. Okay, maybe Mother Teresa and maybe the pope, but that list is short. And then once having determined that you're the 238th call on his list, ask the bundler, "Hey, what's in it for *you*?"

Most of us are so charmed by being given this golden opportunity to get fleeced that we don't ask about the fees or how the deal really works. That would be gauche and déclassé and offensive and rude. He might say, "Do you really think I'm only doing this, giving you this opportunity, because *I* am getting a fee? Do you think I'm so craven and grubby to only think of you because *I'm* going to get rich off you? No! I'm doing this in honor and recognition of our long-standing friendship."

Truth is, he wouldn't recognize you in a crowd of three people, but hey, it's the dance.

The model for the liquor-license program was a simple one. And on the face of it, the purported reliance on Chicago Title as the escrow holder was a powerful inducement. But like any black swan, there's always the possibility that powerful companies can, from time to time, act badly, dishonestly, and even potentially criminally.

If you invested through the PPM, you needed to be an accredited investor.

Accredited is a very important concept, and you can't simply decide on your own that you're accredited. There are a series of questions that the investor must answer truthfully to be classified as an accredited investor. In layman's terms, you're attesting to the fact that you know what you're doing financially, have significant net worth, and aren't living hand-to-mouth in a downtown homeless shelter.

For those of you who delight in financial details, see the following:

> "An accredited investor is an individual or a business entity that is allowed to trade securities that may not be registered with financial authorities. They are entitled to this privileged access by satisfying certain requirements regarding their income, net worth, asset size, governance status or professional experience."

(I am particularly fond of the phrase "privileged access.")

> "In the U.S., the term accredited investor is used by the Securities and Exchange Commission (SEC) under Regulation D to refer to investors who are financially sophisticated and have a reduced need for the protection provided by regulatory disclosure filings. Sellers of unregistered securities are only allowed to sell to accredited investors, who are deemed financially sophisticated enough to bear the risks. Unregistered securities are considered inherently

riskier because they lack the normal disclosures that come
with SEC registration."

But being an accredited investor doesn't protect you; it protects the
promoter—you know, the guy running the deal and taking the fees.
It is his get-out-of-jail-free card, because his defense is "You said you
were financially sophisticated and had traded options on the Chicago
Board of Trade, so don't blame me—*you* should have known better."

As time passes, we'll see how much water that position really holds.
There are also "clawbacks" being initiated at this time by the receiver.
A clawback is a simple concept, designed to prevent you from profit-
ing unfairly. If you received money or a preference or benefited at the
expense of others—that is to say, you got back more money than you
put in, then the receiver wants to knock on your door and politely ask
you to give back your unfair gains, that being the amount greater than
what you invested. However, the part about "politely" often quickly
escalates to a demand and then litigation. In addition to the receiver
clawbacks, there are currently more than eight other lawsuits looking
for any and all the deep pockets, and the part about that long-standing
friendship . . . well, see you in court, pal.

*** ***

CHAPTER 11
Torrey Pines Bank
A near-death experience.

I know that a Ponzi scheme can't work. They work until they don't. Along the way, sometimes there's a near-death experience, an almost "We're dead in the water" moment; and then the wind shifts, someone blinks, and the pirate ship tacks away and keeps going. That moment, when it appears as if all is lost, is the one that terrifies the heart of the promoter, and in return brings forth the most outrageous response, the one that seems to suggest that, in fact, pigs *can* fly.

It is February 2016. My primary bundler, Investor #1, Kim Peterson, has been funneling money into the program for a few years. It was Kim who thought we should call it a *program*. It made it sound like a diet plan or a gym workout or a detox treatment. It was like the investment banker who's explaining a program to make you richer. Who wouldn't sign up for that?

At the beginning of the liquor-license program in spring 2012, Kim was mostly using his own money, but after the first legitimate deals turned a healthy profit, he came to me and said, "What do we have to do to blow this up? I can raise multiple millions, and we need more licenses."

Kim was in that first tranche of six licenses on The Patio on Lamont. I didn't feel too stressed on that one. I figured I could always pay it back, but Kim was pushing. Six licenses were not what he had in mind.

I felt that I could probably handle borrowing a couple of million, but beyond that, there would only be the voice of *The Producers'* Leo Bloom in my ear: "No way out." As I think back, Kim and I were a perfect pair. We had what psychiatrists call "compatible neuroses." His greed matched my weakness. We were made for each other. Fatal attraction.

His model was simple: Kim would borrow money from the bank at 6 percent and put it into liquor-license loans at 16 percent. It was a no-brainer for him to print money. Nice work if you can get it. And to get it, he needed to go to a friendly bank. Why keep messing around with raising small-time money from rich people? After all, it was Willie Sutton who famously explained why he robbed banks: "Because that's where the money is." And so Kim sets off to see the loan officers at San Diego Private Bank (now called CalPrivate Bank), and they agreed to loan him $5 million on a line of credit.

Here's a how a line of credit works: The bank gives you the ability to draw money at your discretion, and in exchange, you sign a personal guarantee that says you promise to pay back the money, plus interest. In addition, a bank might very well ask what you plan to do with the money. So you tell them that you're going to lend money to people seeking liquor licenses, and that the loans are secure and in a safe place at Chicago Title, which is in the business of not only real estate and title insurance, but also, as it says on their website, they provide the Form 226 escrow services for the ABC, the first required step to start the process of applying for a liquor license.

From the Chicago Title website:

> "The applicant, within 30 days of application, shall fur-
> nish ABC with a statement that the purchase price or
> consideration has been deposited in escrow (Form ABC-

226). The applicant shall also submit a copy to the transferor and a copy to the escrow holder."

Seems straightforward enough.

San Diego Private Bank approves the line of credit. Usually a line of credit is extended based on the borrower's net worth and good standing in the community. Kim had both. He could essentially pretty much do what he wanted with the money. The bank never asked to see the escrow agreements.

However, in future transactions with other banks, Kim would bump up against the audacity of those banks wanting to actually see the Form 226 escrow agreements as well. Imagine the outrage! Kim was not a man who took kindly to having his financial integrity impugned.

So Kim got his $5 million, sent it to Chicago in care of the escrow ladies for safe keeping, and then went off on another ski trip.

Kim always dealt directly with Chicago, never through my company, ANI, and voilà, it worked perfectly—his interest/profit was paid like clockwork, so he decided to roll it over and go back to the bank for more.

That is why the three-card monte dealers in New York always make sure that you win the first few rounds. You begin to think you're playing with house money, which you are, until you lose your house.

Kim still had the roof over his head, and he wanted to go bigger, so he returned to the bank for an increase in his line of credit for an additional $7.5 million. So now he and the bank were in for $12.5 million. Kim promised to pay the money back, and in order to ensure that his word is good, he gave them another personal guarantee.

When the program was closed at the end of 2019, CalPrivate Bank sued Kim Peterson and Chicago Title to recover $12.5 million. I was thinking of sending their board of directors the rule book on three-card monte.

But the money from CalPrivate wasn't enough. They were a modest-size bank, and Kim was bumping up against their loan limits. He needed to find bigger fish. But the bigger fish that he went to, like Wells Fargo and Bank of America, told him they didn't understand the program and turned him down. But he kept casting, so he threw a line to Torrey Pines Bank, a local entrepreneurial establishment with a specialty in real estate lending and a long history with Chicago Title, which many of their clients used for their escrow and title work.

Kim was the master negotiator, and he didn't want to scare them off. Begin small, nothing special—just the usual $5 million starter line of credit, if you please. Kim told me that there was a fair amount of back-and-forth, but in the end, they agreed to make the loan, and Kim agreed to personally guarantee it. The guy was handing out guarantees like they were M&Ms.

It's not uncommon for a bank to ask a borrower just what the hell they're planning to do with the bank's money, and while it may not technically be any of the bank's business, their thinking is that since a borrower wants to do business with their bank, they'd like to know just what the borrower's business is.

Kim told them, "Going to make loans secured by liquor licenses, which are in escrow at Chicago Title." And then the bank said they'd like to do a bit more due diligence. They wanted to get more comfortable and see the "backup escrow agreements." Oh, the humanity.

Kim has, from time to time, been characterized as being somewhat volatile, so you can imagine that he might have taken umbrage to this inquiry. *Don't they know who I am?* But the program needed to be fed, and the tranche of 25 licenses was all signed and sealed, ready to go. So he asked me to send the escrow agreements to the bank. And I sent him exactly what he asked for.

But let me be clear: None of those escrow agreements supported a current, active license for sale, and there were no actual applicants for these licenses. However, 25 pieces of paper on Chicago Title letterhead, with what looks exactly like 25 legitimate escrow agreements, show up at the bank signed by "Wendy Reynolds."

So who's Wendy Reynolds? She's a figment of my imagination, a character I created.

The actual escrow officers at Chicago Title at that time were Della DuCharme and Betty Elixman. There *was* no Wendy Reynolds. That name was conjoined by me from a former and beloved escrow officer, Joanne Reynolds, who'd worked for years at Chicago Title. It was Joanne who figured out how to do the Master Escrow Agreement for me.

Della was Joanne's boss, and as my business at Chicago ramped up and significant fees were being paid to Chicago, and then bonuses associated with those fees were being handed out, Joanne, who was doing most of the work, finally went to Della to ask for a raise. Della said no, so Joanne Reynolds packed her bags, walked out the door, and went to work at another escrow and title company.

And now I had a problem. I'd been signing the escrow agreements as Joanne Reynolds, but with Joanne gone, I needed a new name for the escrow signatures. So based on my affection for Joanne, as well as a passing childhood romance with Peter Pan, Ms. Wendy Reynolds was born as the new escrow officer. I think back and can only imagine the shitstorm I would have stirred up if I'd picked Tinker Bell Reynolds.

When Joanne left Chicago, I picked Wendy Reynolds as the new nom de plume because I wanted the continuity of the last name, Reynolds. I knew that the deal guys weren't very detail oriented, and they would most likely simply skim over the name anyway. But seeing the name "Reynolds" could give them comfort, with no reason to be concerned.

After Wendy became familiar with the bundlers, my assistant, Joelle Hanson, would sign for her, but only using the initials "WR." As for Betty, I always signed her name myself, until Joelle came up with the really good idea to have signature stamps made. It was fast, easy, and avoided any potential workers' comp claims for carpal tunnel syndrome. After all, we signed more than a thousand escrow agreements.

As you may know, all banks have an assistant vice president, which is a title you give to any junior nobody who's been with the bank more than three weeks. And Torrey Pines Bank had one; his name was Chris Grassa. It was Kim who told me this story, but after hearing the Keystone Cop sequence of events, the only conclusion that I could come to is that the bank should have made this kid, Grassa, their next CEO. By the way, Kim did not find this as funny as I did.

The loan papers for Kim and his $5 million line of credit were in progress and were heading for approval. Grassa's job was to finalize the details. Kim called and asked me to send Grassa the 25 loan escrow agreements that the bank was considering as collateral for the loan.

I sent them, so Grassa started to finalize the paperwork in preparation to wire funds for the line of credit, and then he stopped for a moment. He just wanted to double-check the wiring instructions. To do that, he called Chicago Title and asked to speak to Wendy Reynolds—after all, it was her name on the bottom of the 25 agreements. He might as well get the facts from the horse's mouth. But he called the main office in Mission Valley, not the downtown office at 7th and B, which is known as the Darth Vader building, where Della and Betty work. A nice lady answered his phone call.

Grassa: "May I please speak to Wendy Reynolds?"

Lady: "Thank you. I will connect you. [There was a pause while our telephone lady looked rapidly through her directory. The pause was longer than usual.] Excuse me, but I can't find that name. Are you sure you want to speak with Wendy Reynolds?"

Grassa: "Yes, Wendy Reynolds, Chicago Title. Maybe she's in the escrow department."

[Another pause, and our operator came back with the death knell.]

Lady: "I've looked carefully, and unfortunately, sir, we have no record of anyone by the name of Wendy Reynolds working here."

Grassa: "Huh. Are you sure? I have some escrows signed by Ms. Reynolds, and I need to speak with her."

Lady: "I'm new here, so let me send you to HR [human resources]; they may have better information."

And so, Grassa moved to HR, where again he was met with a very polite denial.

HR lady: "We do not have a Wendy Reynolds in our database. No one by that name."

Grassa: "I think she's in escrow."

At this point the Chicago lady was doing duck-and-dodge 2.0. She knew nothing.

HR lady: "Okay, let me send you to the escrow department at the downtown office. They may have the information you need."

Grassa: "Thank you."

The phone rang downtown, and Betty Elixman answered his phone call.

Grassa: "Can I please speak with Wendy Reynolds? I need to verify the wiring instructions for Mr. Kim Peterson's loan."

If I were writing this scene in a movie, this would be the time where a black gloved hand reached up and cut the power, the lights went out, a door slammed shut, the alarms were disabled, and the "scepter" was stolen from the vault. Maybe add some rain beating on the windows.

The only reason Grassa was calling to speak to Wendy Reynolds was to verify the wiring instructions. He wasn't questioning the escrows; he was simply calling because of his concern about the potential for fraudulent wire transfers.

Now Betty may not have been the brightest bulb, but she was a team player, a good soldier. She wasn't exactly sure what was happening, but she moved the ball to the main lady, Della.

Betty: "I think she's in escrow; let me send you over there to my supervisor. Please hold."

Elixman quickly transferred Grassa to Della DuCharme, who didn't miss a beat. She told Grassa that Ms. Reynolds must be either a new employee or an outside contractor in a different building, but regardless, "ANI is my client, and I will gladly verify the wiring instructions," which she did. Grassa said thank you, hung up, and Della immediately sent me a text.

Now my game plan was always the same with the girls; it was set in stone. If there were any hiccups, Della was to send me a text, and I would get on it immediately. Her text came, short and sweet, with actually only one word: *"Urgent."* This was followed by a second text in caps: *"CALL ME. WHO IS WENDY REYNOLDS?"*

At that very moment in time, Kim was skiing in Japan. I mean, come on, you're expecting a $5 million loan and you can't be bothered to stick around just in case, but no, you'd rather be skiing 6,000 miles away when someone calls looking for a Wendy Reynolds. That behavior was somewhere between Steve McQueen way cool and Dumb and Dumber, absolute stupidity. You be the judge.

When the text came in, I was walking on the beach in Coronado on my monthly stroll with my longtime friend and mentor, Alan Robbins, a former state senator in California from 1974 to 1991. He'd gotten into some trouble and pleaded guilty to federal racketeering and income-tax evasion charges in connection with the "Shrimpscam" scandal (federal agents claimed to represent a shrimp company that offered bribes to lawmakers in return for their support on legislation at the Capitol). He was sentenced to five years, and served 18 months at Lompoc federal prison.

I was very aware that this was a seminal moment in our program. Della had no idea who Wendy Reynolds was, but she also knew for sure that there was no Wendy Reynolds in the escrow department of Chicago Title. I made a simple, and in my mind, completely rational decision. I told her that Wendy Reynolds was a fictitious person. She did not exist.

You can appreciate that this might have caused a mild shock to the system, but to Della's credit, she barely blinked.

Again, if I were writing the movie, this would be the moment where the suspect says to the detective, "Yeah, that's my gun, and yes, those are my fingerprints on the fireplace poker, and yes, the dead body on the carpet is my brother-in-law, but I can explain everything."

Della picked up the phone call and simply said one word to me: "So?"

And I told her in a matter-of-fact voice—with no alarm, no urgency, and no concern—that Wendy Reynolds was the name I was using on all the escrows for Kim.

"Della, I only use that name for the Kim escrows so he'll never call you up and bug you. I'm simply trying to be thoughtful and protect you from being aggravated by the guy. You know how difficult he can be."

And Della says to me, "Well, I figured as much." End of story.

Sure, now we can put the dead body into the trunk of the car and dump it in the East River.

The 25 escrows that Peterson presented to Torrey Pines Bank had, in fact, been signed by me, using the name Wendy Reynolds. I concede that signing a made-up name made no sense. As I look back on this moment, I think it was my unconscious way of trying to find a way out, a way to stop the madness. I kept leaving bread crumbs, and it seemed as if no one wanted to pick them up. I guess I wasn't strong enough to stop it myself—I didn't have the willpower—but if someone had come along to call me on it, I think I would have gladly handed them the keys. It was me asking for 50 ways to leave my lover, but I couldn't seem to find even one.

Kim liked to be in control of his own program, and he was the only one who could initiate the wiring instructions for the bank. Everything went through him. I immediately send him a text at 10:00 a.m. Wednesday suggesting that there might be a minor hiccup in his loan approval. It was 1:00 a.m. on Thursday in Japan, but soon he would have more news to consider with his morning coffee.

He'd gotten a text from Robert Casey, who was the in-house principal legal adviser to the executive team at Torrey Pines Bank. His text was more succinct than mine: *"Call me."*

While Kim was sleeping, Casey had called Della to ask for some clarification. Torrey Pines Bank was a major real estate lender and had deep ties with Chicago Title, where their clients did a large amount of their title and escrow work. He asked Della, "What's going on over there?"

Della told him, "I'm not sure, Bob; it must have something to do with Kim Peterson. I don't really know the situation. Kim is part of Gina's liquor-license program [This is the Sergeant Schultz defense: "I know nothing."] But if you have any concerns, why not just give him a call. All I did was give your man there the wiring instructions."

Casey sent his text. And then he called Kim.

When the phone rang, Kim was asleep, so he fumbled for the phone in the dark and saw that he didn't recognize the number, so he answered it with a bit of trepidation—after all, it was 4:00 a.m. in Japan. He probably wondered who'd died.

Casey asked him about the 25 escrows at the bank, signed by someone who apparently didn't exist, and then he told Kim that at this time, they're becoming disinclined to make the loan. No soup for you.

But Kim Peterson was not a man to be trifled with. He told Casey in so many words, "Do you know who I am? Do you know who you're dealing with? Do you know who my lawyers are?"

Casey was polite and backed off a bit. So Kim said he would get to the bottom of this, clear everything up, and get right back to him. He told Casey that it was probably only a minor misunderstanding. He said something to the effect of: "I'll get in touch with Wendy and get you what you need. I'm counting on that loan."

And then he called me. Let the screaming and the finger-pointing with that sawed-off digit begin.

After the first wave of WTF and confusion, he said, "Talk to your girls, find out who this damn Wendy Reynolds is, figure out what's going on, and get back to me."

I waited 30 minutes, enough time for Kim to believe I'd made some phone calls, and then I called him back. I told him that Della had just begun subbing some of his work to an outside 1099 contractor because he was generating so much paperwork. He required a lot of specific hand-holding, and Della wanted to be sure to meet his needs efficiently. I explained to Kim that this new contractor must have gotten confused and signed her own name instead of Della's. And that's why Chicago Title HR had no record of her "as an employee."

Kim replied, "Well, okay, but I need Della to fix the escrows and get them back to the bank so they'll complete the deal."

I said, "No problem. I'll have Della get it cleared up and have the escrows sent to the bank."

I reminded Kim that Chicago was doing this Master Escrow holding account as a favor to me. They didn't do these any longer. And the paperwork he was creating for Della was sometimes too much, so she was using this new person up in Orange County to sign the documents for her on his accounts.

So there you have it. It was the classic "It's really all your fault, and furthermore, you're lucky to be in the program." And the fact that my answer to him was ridiculous and irrational didn't seem to faze him.

As I've said before, greed is a powerful emotion, sometimes leading to blindness.

But Kim was determined to get his money, so the next day he called Torrey Pines and spoke to Grassa. He was going to try to convince him to go ahead with the wire. Grassa politely listened and replied that he fully understood, and that he was sure that it was nothing more than a minor paperwork mix-up, but he would still really like to speak with Wendy Reynolds.

Kim: "You still want to speak to Ms. Reynolds?"

Grassa: "If that wouldn't be too much trouble."

This is the moment when Kim had to take a deep breath and pause carefully, what psychologist/economist Daniel Kahneman calls "thinking fast and slow." But Kim didn't get to be a big shot by whiffing on the game winner.

Kim: "Look, why don't I just have Chicago send you 25 new escrow agreements, with Della's signature, to replace the other ones, and we'll be good to go."

Now, banks like fees. Grassa went to Casey, and Casey still wanted to do the deal, but he wanted the file to be nice and clean, so he called Tom Schwiebert, a senior vice president at Chicago Title, and suggested that perhaps an "incumbency certificate" would meet their needs.

An incumbency certificate is an official document issued by a corporation that lists the names of who holds what positions within an organization and "is most frequently used to confirm the identity of individuals who are authorized to enter into legally binding transactions on behalf of the company."

So I went to see Schwiebert myself, as I needed to tie up loose ends. I took him out for a couple of drinks and told him how important Della was to Chicago, and what a terrific employee she was. I told him about all the new business that would be coming his way (as well as tickets to the private box at the Padres games), and while he wasn't thrilled about signing anything, incumbency thy name is Schwiebert.

Now, Della was able to sign all 25 escrow agreements in place of Wendy; and in effect, Peterson and the Torrey Pines Bank deal got a do-over. Della signed the escrows in the lobby of Chicago Title. We never did business together in her office, only in the lobby, sitting in those nice Mies Van der Rohe chairs.

The only time we didn't use the lobby was when a major new player, Ovation Finance, first got involved in the platform; they initially did call Della on her speakerphone—with me standing over her shoulder, right behind her in her office. I knew when the call was coming; it had been orchestrated, and I didn't want to leave anything to chance. Otherwise, it was all lobby, all the time.

So, finally it was time to close Torrey. Della has signed all 25 escrows, delivered them to Grassa, and the fat lady was about to sing. Kim was calling, but I told him that we were all good and that he should go back out and hit those double-black diamonds.

I knew the guy loved to ski, but I wondered if he ever considered flying home for $5 million.

That whirlwind felt to me like the final scenes in *The Wizard of Oz*. The Wicked Witch of the West had a magical broomstick that she used to fly, and when Dorothy melted the witch, she took the broomstick and used it as proof that the witch was dead. Delivering the escrows, properly signed, to Torrey Pines Bank was, in my mind, the broomstick.

But there were a few loose strands of straw in that broomstick that I hadn't accounted for.

The transmittal email that I used to communicate to the bank with respect to the new 25 escrow agreements was sent from the email IP domain address @ChicagoTitleandEscrows.com. Just as a point of information, the correct, legal IP address for Chicago Title is @ CTT.com. I'd created this different email domain earlier in the year just for Kim, in case he came up with some bright new idea to make more money.

Grassa noticed the new email address and saw that it wasn't the correct one for Chicago Title. You had to like this guy—he was relentlessly detailed. That's why I suggested earlier that he should be the new CEO of the bank.

Grassa called Kim to ask why the email address on the transmittal seemed different. Kim had no idea, but he was back from Japan, wound up, pissed off, wanted his money, and he did what people do when they're pissed off: he went to see his attorney.

Scott Wolfe, a Harvard Law graduate, was a very powerful lawyer at a giant law firm, Latham and Watkins. He represented Kim in various other endeavors, and he was equally outraged that his client was being held up to such scrutiny. He told Kim that large corporations often have multiple email addresses and that this second email address seemed harmless and perfectly legitimate. And he was prepared to talk to Casey if need be.

But there was one more twist coming. Grassa, the junior sleuth, was suspicious about the transmittal email address, and on his own initiative went to the California Department of Corporations database and looked up the company called Chicago Title and Escrows, LLC. And he found that the registered owner of that company was me!

This is the place in the movie where the detective finds the dead body in the trunk with the murder weapon and your fingerprints, and confronts the driver, Mr. Kim Peterson, with incontrovertible evidence: "Hey, what do you know about this dead body?"

Peterson says that this is *not* my car, and I've never seen that dead body before in my life, and even if it *were* my car, and even if that dead body *looked* like Gina Champion-Cain, I assure you that there's a perfectly good reason why there's this confusion about email addresses and owners, and I'll be back to you in a jiffy with some answers just as soon as I can get on down the road to another bank.

And instead of calling out the dead body to his superiors, our junior sleuth just shuts the trunk and goes back to the office. Again, nobody blinked. Torrey Pines Bank never made the loan, and only after Kim threatened to sue him did they return his deposit..

There was fraud, forgery, and flimflam, but nobody said another word about it. Kim went on to raise multiple millions of dollars, and the program wasn't flagged by the SEC until May 2019. Chicago Title just kept receiving money, taking fees, opening and closing mythical escrows, and liquor licenses appeared and disappeared.

Kim, at this moment, reminded me of Kasper Gutman (the character known as the "Fat Man" in the *Maltese Falcon*): "If we must spend another year on the quest . . . well, sir, it will be an additional expenditure of time of only . . . five-and-fifteenth-seventeenths percent."

There's always another bank around the corner.

*** ***

CHAPTER 12
Fake Escrow Companies and More

Keyser Soze and the usual suspects.

One of the largest bundlers for the program was Kim Funding, LLC. Kim was a very early investor in the liquor-license lending program—he was so early that he was part of the first group that did several of the original legitimate loans, the real licenses that had real applicants who needed to borrow money to fund real escrows pursuant to ABC 226.

Attorney Bill Adams, aka Wonder Boy, was the conduit to the majority of the liquor-license brokers who had buyers and sellers in that arena. I knew Bill, and he arranged the first couple of legitimate applicants. But Kim was wearing rose-colored glasses, and he wanted to go big, so I had to go visit Wonder Boy and search for more licenses. It was at that meeting that Bill explained that there were just not that many licenses floating around. There was no central database. So he could do a couple, but he couldn't do a few hundred.

I look back on that meeting, and I'm very sorry I took it. It was the first few turns down a double-black-diamond ski slope, and I was unaware that I was about to trigger an avalanche that would ultimately bury me.

But let's go back a bit and take one more look at the snow on that mountain.

November 2012

The Patio on Lamont opened its doors and was standing room only. I looked in the mirror above the bar and staring back at me was the Queen of Lamont.

I wonder now if maybe one restaurant and a couple vacation rentals would have been enough. I could have stopped right then and there. But as you know, I didn't. The puzzle of how much is enough is the Rubik's Cube of life.

But I needed the $600,000 to finish the restaurant, and Kim wanted licenses, so I kept turning the cube. The martini shakers were shaking, but if you shake too much, you might accidentally trigger that avalanche.

I always figured that if the snow started to shift only a little bit, I could always pay back the $600,000. I could handle that. I saw it as nothing more than a short-term bridge loan. So I pushed off the top and did a couple elegant turns down the mountain.

March 2016

Unfortunately, it seems to be human nature that when you have a good thing going, the next thing people want to do is muck around and try to screw it up. They'll tell you that they're tweaking it to improve it, but you and I know that's a lie.

A couple hundred million had gone in and out at Chicago Title by this time. The program was just humming along, so Kim came to me with an idea of how to make the fly wheel spin faster and spit out a few more dollars per second.

You remember that domain @ChicagoTitleEscrows.com? It was Kim who had the genius idea that what the world really needed was another escrow company, just in case Chicago started to go sideways or get cold feet.

Chicago Title is owned by Fidelity National Title Insurance, which is a very large company. It has annual revenues of about $8.5 billion. As mentioned previously, the email of its subsidiary, Chicago Title Insurance Company, was @CTT.com. As also mentioned, there was also a smaller company called Chicago Title and Escrows, LLC. It was a very small company. It had no revenue. It had no employees. It had no office. However, it did have an email address, @ChicagoTitle Escrows.com. That company and the email address were owned by me.

Kim had been complaining for years about Chicago Title and their fees. He was always thinking of ways to make more money for himself. He figured that if Chicago was making so much money, then why weren't they treating us better?

In retrospect, I should have told him to leave well enough alone and stop aggravating the shit out of me, and "Could you keep your hands out of my kitchen, you greedy bastard?" But I didn't. My own thinking was that Chicago was treating us really well, money went in and came out easily enough, and so what if they charged heavy fees? Who else was going to do this for us?

Kim always wanted more control. He always felt he was being slighted. He wanted more direct access, but I was the wedge between him and Della and Betty. I protected them from his wrath.

I remembered that Kim was on the board of directors at the Bishop's School, an expensive private school in La Jolla. It was an exclusive group, and Kim's personality was such that he was always in financial competition with the other board members.

Making more money was important for him, and his view of himself—and money—had the added benefit of securing his seat at the table. You needed to be able to raise your paddle at the fundraisers. But no matter what he had, I think he was always haunted by the fact that the other guy's plane was bigger.

And so he came to me with a totally insane, half-baked idea to inter-view other title companies to see if we could get a better deal. He was moving millions every month, and he wanted to try and save a penny. This was a serious conflict in our relationship. I went to see him and read him the riot act. It was only because of Bill Adams and Joanne Reynolds that we even had a Master Escrow Account. That ship had sailed, never to come to port again. Stop the madness.

But Kim kept pointing that damn stub at me, demanding that I at least look around. Okay, anything to shut him up, so I went to Stewart Title, but they had no interest. In fact, they were a tiny bit suspicious, asking why we'd be leaving Chicago, and could I explain more. That fed into *my* own paranoia, and I began to consider that maybe Chicago would bail on us one day.

The next stop was First American Title. They had concerns; the words *money laundering* floated in the air for a moment. They passed. The thought that it might be a Ponzi scheme never crossed their minds.

Who knows when or if Della's boss, Tom Schwiebert, would stop looking the other way? We had the one Master Escrow with millions flopping in and out, but it never "closed," and that was a definite red flag that someone at Chicago would see if they ever bothered to look.

I reported back to Kim, and he pushed for a backup plan. He decided that what we needed was our own escrow company. That way we could keep all the fees. This was insanity, plain and simple.

I took his stub and pointed out to him that the only reason our deal worked is that Chicago was one of the largest title and escrow com-panies in the world, and that the investors felt safe with their money there. If you told them to wire $500,000 to a two-bit, fly-by-night, never-heard-of-them-before escrow company, with a single office in a suburban strip mall under a freeway, they would laugh in your face. And then if you told them that we were the owners of the escrow company, our investors would have run for the hills, only stopping for a moment to see their lawyer and have us committed.

I told him that nobody would give us a dime, ever.

Kim sat quietly for a moment, a behavior that wasn't typical for him. I could see that he was thinking hard, pondering the issue. "Well, you might be right, but Chicago does take a lot of fees, and we both know that maybe one day, you never know, just in case . . ." *So you just keep thinking, Butch, that's what you're good at.*

I went on the internet and searched for any available name that had the word *Chicago* in it, just wondering if they'd left some crumbs on the table that an enterprising entrepreneur could pick up.

And then, the three lemons showed up. There it was: Chicago Escrow and Title, Inc.—available to be plucked from the ether, and voilà, courtesy of Legal Zoom and GoDaddy, I had a new company with a nice new EIN (employer identification number). All nice, tidy, and legal in October 2016.

I did create an email address for that corporation, but I never opened a bank account. Kim was thinking that if we had an escrow company and that if the wires went to something that had the words *Chicago* and *escrows* in the transmittal, people wouldn't even bother to look. I thought he was out of his mind. But here's the truth: it turns out later that he was right.

February 2017

It was the time of the famous "Wendy Reynolds" debacle at Torrey Pines Bank. But let's go back for a moment and remember how the whole thing came crashing down. Torrey Pines Bank executive Chris Grassa had received the final transmittal email from me along with the 25 escrows, delivered to the bank. He noticed the email address, and it seemed strange to him: @chicagotitleescrows.com. A curious fellow, he went searching for the incorporation statement attached to the email, and he came up with an LLC that had been formed four months ago, called Chicago Escrow and Title, LLC; the Agent of Service for that company was none other than little old me.

And then the floodgates opened. But don't you love the irony of the whole thing. Admittedly, I did use the wrong email address by accident (or at least I told myself that it was by accident), but that email would never have existed if Kim hadn't pushed so hard to have another escrow company, if he hadn't obsessed about the interest payments we weren't getting on our deposits from Chicago. Greed will get you every time. There's a certain justice to unintended consequences.

Kim, you were sick of paying them the fees and you wanted interest on the money, and you told me to set up a company in case Chicago Title couldn't do this anymore. So I set it up just like you asked, Kim. I did it for you. Isn't that what everyone says during the divorce proceedings?

I later heard through the grapevine that Kim came back to see Casey and Grassa, and he was standing in the lobby of Torrey Pines Bank with two boxes filled with escrow agreements signed by Wendy Reynolds. He was waving them around trying to prove that Wendy existed in an alternate universe. He was like King Lear on the rocks railing at the gods. The receptionist finally had to call security. You know, I'm just not completely sure why I used that old email address anyway. Was it commission or omission?

Kim called me the next day and demanded that I shut down the LLC "with the confusing name." *Of course, Kim, whatever you wish. Just remember how it came to pass.* I didn't want to piss him off completely, so I sent him the documents that proved the LLC was canceled.

And ironically, after about a week, Kim came to me to say that all was forgiven. Mistakes happen, and there was always another bank. I guess that was his way of saying he couldn't quit me.

However, because of the Torrey Pines incident, there was heat in the kitchen at Chicago Title, and Della got a note from her big boss, Joe Goodman. He expressed his concern about the Torrey fiasco to her, and then he gave her some blah blah blah and finally told her to go ahead with the Gina program, but just "be careful and tread lightly."

One could reasonably conclude that Chicago's management operated mostly with benign neglect when it came to the girls and me. For his part, Kim was still agitated, but I calmed him down. There was the tension between wanting to yell at me versus killing the goose laying the golden eggs for him. As for the other bundlers, well, Chicago never said a word, so it was business as usual for the others.

It's fair to say that after the Torrey Pines affair, the boat was rocked hard, but the mast didn't fall down, so back under sail, Kim goes to see the Banc of California with the program, but this time, no chump-change $5 million; he wanted $25–$30 million. It was the same amount of work.

Okay, I admit that Plan B had some issues. It was the summer of 2017, and I got to thinking that maybe a new corporation might be a nice place to receive the wires, just in case. So Plan C was born. I went looking again, and once again, three lemons—there it was: Chicago Escrows and T, Inc., and this time I opened an account at Chase Bank. The name wasn't as good as the first one, but close enough, and beggars can't be choosers.

And sure enough, in the latter part of 2017, several investors begin to wire money into the account at Chase Bank. No one, including Kim, seemed to notice that Chicago Escrows and T, Inc., was not the real Chicago Title. All they ever asked was: "Where do I send the wire?" It's always satisfying when a backup plan comes together.

The first monies that came into the Chase account were from California Opportunity License Fund, LLC, my old friend Ilan Awerbuch. But not in a straight line. Well, not exactly. Ilan had very strong feelings, so he always sent his money to his own bank at Wells Fargo; and then my controller, Cris Torres, would transfer the money from Wells to Chase. It struck me as needlessly complicated. But Ilan liked it, since in this way, he could avoid wire-transfer fees and earn interest on the money. I have from time to time wondered at these financial geniuses who were moving millions and continued to worry about pennies. I know that a penny earned is a penny saved, but I also know about not being able to see the forest for the trees.

But one of the bundlers *did* raise an eyebrow. Dave Sider (Synapse Group) came to me at one point to ask why his money was going to an account at Chase, instead of Chicago. And I needed a good answer, so I told him that the Chase account was a subsidiary money market account that Della had set up just for me so that investors like him could collect interest on his money. The money was still there for Chicago; they were just doing this so we could collect interest, which was something that Chicago didn't normally do. Della was doing it as an "experiment."

I explained to Sider that there were some rules about interest, and that we couldn't just keep taking money out to pay his fees. We needed to earn some interest along the way. I told him it was a way for Chicago to get around the rules.

When I gave wiring instructions to Sider and a few of the other bundlers, I didn't put Chicago Escrows and T on the instructions; I used the name Chicago Escrows and Title, the old corporation that had been created for Kim and then was dissolved. But the damnedest thing was when the investors wired their money to Chase Bank, and even though the wires were clearly mislabeled with the wrong corporate name, the bank still deposited the money.

Chase liked fees the same as everyone else. The fact that the account had the wrong name didn't seem to raise the slightest bit of concern. As I look back now, it's hard to fully grasp the number of enablers that knowingly participated in this $400 million Ponzi scheme. Like a theatrical farce with a half dozen doors, there were so many people looking the other way that it's a miracle that no one saw anyone else and that they didn't bump into each other on their way in and out.

The combined greed and stupidity of the participants across all levels was almost beyond belief. I was waiting to stop the madness if anyone had taken the time to call me on it.

This Chase bank account remained active until May 2019, when the SEC sent its first subpoena. When the receiver took over that account, $2 million was still in it.

*** ***

CHAPTER 13

A Day in the Life

"You only live once, but if you do it right, once is enough." —Mae West

I was a working girl.

My mornings always started off the same. I would get up early every day around 4:30 a.m., so that's why the 5:00 a.m. wake-up call here in prison is a no-brainer for me. I would read the *San Diego Union-Tribune*, the *New York Times*, and the *Wall Street Journal* with my morning coffee. A little gardening outside, then shower, dress, eat (eggs, bacon, pancakes, and so on—I like a big breakfast), and then head out with the dogs to each of the various businesses that needed my attention that day.

My first stop was always Marina Village in Mission Beach, where there's a large patch of grass for the dogs to catch the ball, sniff, and run around. We would always go look at the waves at the jetty after that, grab another coffee at Swell Cafe in Mission Beach, and then head on over to the corporate headquarters at 3515 Hancock Street.

We had 50 employees on-site at corporate (everyone else was in the field, either at stores, restaurants, or the various satellite offices we had around the city), so I'd stop by and say hi to every one of them. Then, the same as any CEO, I would do the mail, sign papers, delegate stuff, and then around 11:00 a.m., I'd head to meetings or community events.

Josie, the daughter of Joey Himmelberg—my closest friend—would take charge of the dogs and bring them home around 3:30 p.m. It was crushing when Joey died of a massive heart attack at age 49. We were kindred spirits on Mission Beach—him on his surfboard—so the truth is, I can never really leave my roots. Sometimes watching the waves, I think I can see him out there on the horizon.

Then I'd usually go to lunch and make the rounds of the businesses I hadn't visited in the morning.

I spent very little, if any, time on the liquor-license program. The daily in and out of money and dealing with Chicago Title was handled by Joelle Hanson and Cris Torres. I would meet each of the bundlers only a couple of times per year. Give them an accounting, a glass of wine, and that was it. The primary aggravation for me was Kim Peterson. He required the most hand-holding and was the "neediest" of the group.

By 4:30 p.m., I would head home to meet Steve, who got home around 4:00 from his job in Tijuana, and then I'd either cook or we'd go out to a restaurant. Nothing fancy—we'd either eat at a competitor's place or go to one of our own.

Four times a year, I'd drive up the coast to Carmel-by-the-Sea with the dogs and spend three weeks there. I got a lot of work done while out of town, such as new concepts for the restaurants and retail outlets. And, of course, a little golf with Steve on the weekends.

The other getaway was our house in Rancho Mirage in the Palm Springs area. Steve was in heaven there with the golf—36 holes per day sometimes. There was the pool and the dogs and the good food. We didn't have a boat or a plane or fancy jewelry (okay, I did have *one* nice piece) or an expensive car. The money I took out of the Chicago Title Master Escrow Account was used to support and grow the various enterprises I'd begun. As crazy as it may seem, after the fact,

I had a clear plan to bundle everything up, take the entire company public, and pay back every dime plus more.

One investor floated the idea that I had a secret Swiss bank account with millions stashed away. Nice idea for a movie, but in real life, nope. I didn't even have a Swiss watch.

*** ***

CHAPTER 14

On the Road to Why

If I knew then what I know now, I would have
stopped with one restaurant, one husband,
and three dogs.

I 'm often asked how I chose the businesses that I did.

In 2011, I was trying to "reinvent" myself after the massive fraud
of Cosmopolitan Square, a proposed condominium development
project in downtown San Diego), which took my partners (Peter
Boermeester, now deceased, as well as Steve Corrington) and me on
a roller-coaster ride to the brink of financial ruin. We'd tied up the
land, gotten approvals, and went looking for financing in all the wrong
places, and then ended up being defrauded by a group in Florida (a
Ponzi scheme run by a Greek national known in the States as "John
Condo"), who hustled developers with the promise that they'd fund
your project if you paid them fees up front. (I know that at this point,
I should audition for a role in the next movie, *Dumb and Dumber 2.0.*)

As I took my daily walks on Mission Beach, I kept thinking, *What
do I want to do next in my career?* I was sick of the ups and downs of
ground-up real estate development, although real estate was pretty
deep in my blood.

When my girlfriends came to town, we rented vacation condos at the beach. They were run badly, had few amenities, and didn't allow dogs, but that was what the market offered at that time. What you basically got was a dump facing the Pacific Ocean.

So I came up with a plan to offer a vacation-rental business that would be somewhat unique (remember, this was 2011, prior to the boom of Airbnb rentals)—one that would offer completely renovated beach bungalows that were dog- and kid-friendly, a true family-vacation destination for either San Diego "staycationers" or out-of-town tourists. The term *Luv Surf* came to mind, so I hired a graphic-designer friend to create the logo—one with a dog bone in the surfboard, with clouds and waves. I trademarked it and bought my first cottage (a dump at 727 Windemere Court in Mission Beach) in late 2011 through a lender who'd taken it back in foreclosure. I convinced the bank to give me 100 percent financing, and then used my own cash to renovate the place, including an outside shower to wash your feet and your dog.

I was back in business.

And then I found *another* dump to renovate, and I did the same program again. Luv Surf was rolling. And then I found Lamont, and I could begin to see what a hospitality brand might look like. Stay at the beach and eat at The Patio.

As I contemplate my life now, the question I ask myself is: *Would one restaurant and a few vacation rentals have been enough?* This was a moment when maybe I should have left well enough alone, but that didn't seem to be in my DNA. What *is* enough is a demon we all have to face.

Another business came about because I was having coffee at my favorite café, Swell. I knew the owner, who was struggling, and I got way ahead of my skis over a double latte that same afternoon I agreed to buy in to his operation. Due diligence was not on the table. I had a vision: grow the place into a local brand where we would roast our own beans, sourced from an organic family farm in South America.

Now I would house people at the beach (with beans and a grinder in each unit), caffeinate them at Swell, and feed them at The Patio.

Next, a building came up for sale. Surf shops were strong, so I bought the building (another SBA 504 loan), whipped up a cute logo, and opened up a retail outlet to sell the Luv Surf lifestyle: hats, T-shirts, the basics.

We had a following, and we got our surf line approved to be in Nordstrom and Urban Outfitter. Success was looming. People loved our stuff. Then I got into a trademark/logo dispute with the owner of another surf place: Heart Surf. In retrospect, who the hell cared about a logo, but I was stupid; fought over nothing; and wasted money, time, lawyers, and ego. And, of course, Nordstrom wouldn't take us on until the trademark dispute was over. And when it *was* over, all that was left was ashes. I was blinded by ego and bad business decisions on that one.

As a note here, one thing I'd never had was a solid mentor, an adviser, a consigliere. If I'd had someone who could have guided me when I was out of control, I probably would not be telling this story from prison.

Next up was building another Patio restaurant on Goldfinch near downtown. Then one day I was at home watching a Michigan football game and the phone rang. A nice lady wanted to know if I'd like to buy her pizza business. She said she needed to sell because she'd recently been diagnosed with an allergy to flour. (I know that sounds crazy, but it was true.) I agreed to meet her the next Sunday, and by halftime of the Detroit Lions game that day, I'd agreed to do the deal.

I was now the proud owner of Surf Rider Pizza. It was cash-flowing and had a beer-and-wine license. The Patio served flatbreads that we bought from an outside supplier, so instead, I started making them at the pizza joint, saved money, and improved the product. I was thinking vertical integration.

But it was clear that I was becoming an addict and couldn't leave the "deal" business alone. When Saska's, a famous, long-standing San

Diego restaurant, came up for sale, I bought it without even a second thought about the economics. I had an emotional attachment to the place, but sometimes dumb luck prevails. I didn't touch anything, and the restaurant continued to print money.

I envisioned multiple Patio-Express restaurants in office-building lobbies (I had a deal with Irvine Company for one of their buildings). If I had enough time, I thought I could either sell the whole bundle or take it public, and voilà, before anyone saw that we hadn't really cut the lady in half, pay everyone back—plus. And although that was a fantastical idea, it's equally true that I made some major judgment errors along the way. And since I'm going to be in prison a while, let me share them with you in an effort to prevent other entrepreneurs from making the same ones.

For example, one bad decision was venturing into Petaluma in Northern California. I wanted to "show them" that I could do more than just San Diego County. *Stupid.* Why go to a place where you don't have any connections or understand the local nuances? I bought a building in Petaluma with another SBA 540 loan and started Chicken Pharm. The building had been the first pharmacy in town. Half the building was going to be a shared office space, like WeWork, and the other half was going to sell chicken. Tell that story at a pitch-fest and you'd be laughed out of the room. I would have done better just reopening the pharmacy and giving people a coupon for Kentucky Fried.

The irony is that the receiver ended up selling the whole thing for a large profit. But it was still stupid.

Bad bedfellows. I was going to launch "Front Porch/Luxury Farms" to sell ready-to-eat, gourmet take-out. Okay, the idea had some merit, but then I chose a former *Baywatch* extra who'd married a wealthy Arab Hollywood producer and then got a settlement in her divorce, to be my partner. She'd never run a business in her whole life. Litigation ensued, and I lost money.

My desire to "show them" fueled the madness in these deals. As I wander around the "yard" here in prison, I can see clearly that I was out of control; I needed an intervention. And when I get out, I'm going to be a mentor to younger women to prevent them from making the same stupid mistakes. It's all about behavioral economics: why people do stupid things that aren't in their own best self-interest. In other words, cognitive biases. I'm rereading some books by psychologist/economist Daniel Kahneman while I'm here in prison. If I'd had *him* as an adviser, I probably wouldn't be here.

*** ***

CHAPTER 15
Big Tony
Every woman needs one, just in case.

All of us meet interesting people during our lives. They come and go and intersect, and a few of them make a huge impact. One of my big influences was "Big Tony." We met in the mid-1990s at the downtown San Diego Bodyworks gym. I had a Brazilian jiujitsu instructor working me over, and he kept getting a little too close—you know, brushing my breasts or grabbing my ass—always in an effort to "improve" my exercise routine. But, come on, we all know what's going on.

And then suddenly, this Black guy comes up to the instructor, grabs his shirt, almost picks him up with one hand, and suggests very politely and in a soft-spoken voice, "You need to leave that little one alone." And that was how 6'3" Big Tony and I became acquainted.

He liked cigars and wine, and so did I, and we became friendly. The Churchill's Cigar Lounge in Old Town was a Friday ritual. Tony was a true entrepreneur—he ran a limousine business at the time with a fleet of ten cars and drivers. He was pals with several of the San Diego Charger football players, in particularly, Junior Seau, who was a Hall of Fame linebacker and beloved by the city. He drove for Junior. And that's how he built his business. He ran with some big dogs. And then he ended up driving for me. But how that happened— well, as I've said before, you can't make this stuff up.

Tony grew up in New York City, one of seven children. It was the classic and common tale of overcoming adversity. He was left on his grandmother's doorstep by his biological mother when he was three, and he was raised by his grandma. Hard times and a hard neighborhood, but he survived and ultimately triumphed. I saw him as an underdog and less advantaged, and I wanted to help. I've always liked underdogs.

***

One afternoon after a $25 cigar and a bottle of wine . . . well, I'll let Tony tell the story.

> "I grew up in New York, got through high school, and entered the Marines out here in San Diego. I get out and am doing some construction work. I'm walking home one afternoon and I see a limousine in front of a high-rise office building downtown. I'd never been in a limousine. A guy comes running out the front door, nice suit, must be a lawyer. He's late to do something, and he looks at me and asks if I have a driver's license. Of course, I do. And then he tells me that he'll pay me $100 if I'll go to the airport and pick up some lady.

> "In New York, this kind of thing can get you shot, but in San Diego, WTF, I'm all in. Turns out he had the limo because that's how some client paid him. It was *Lincoln Lawyer* shit, I'm telling you. I do the job, I get paid, and the guy gives me his card and asks for mine. I don't have a business card, but I scribble my number on a piece of paper, and we're all good.

> "And then about a week later, I get a call from the same lawyer to pick up a lady who needs to go to Los Angeles.

She gets in the car, and it turns out to be Gina from the gym. She's going to meet with Dan Aykroyd, a partner in the House of Blues. One thing leads to another—that's the way with Gina. We become friends, and by the time we get back to San Diego, she's got me thinking about starting my own limousine company. The whole thing is crazy, but it's the truth."

On the way home back to San Diego, I asked Tony, "Why are you driving for this lawyer in his limousine? Why don't you get one of your own, start your own company, and run your own show?" So, bang, I lend him a couple dollars, and voilà: Limousines by Anthony, corner of Kettner and Beech in Little Italy.

A classic entrepreneur, street smart, Tony learned quickly. With the name Anthony, he comes up first in the search box. Within two years, he has ten limousines, 13 employees, 50 to 70 regular customers, and is netting $15,000 per month. Besides the NFL guys, he gets some San Diego Padres baseball players and then some real estate developers, and he's starting to live large. Some of his best clients are the criminal defense attorneys who hang out at the Cigar Lounge. It's a crazy place filled with pals, promoters, schemers, and hangers-on, as well as some of the better-known local criminal defense attorneys. Tony is in his element; the lawyers all want him because then they don't have to look for parking while they go in and out of the various hearings and courtrooms.

Long tables, lots of beer and wine, and clouds of expensive smokers every Friday afternoon. Guys come in with small metal suitcases filled with 75 to 100 cigars. They discuss things, show off, trade, and puff. Tony fit in like a glove, albeit an extra-large. His business was good, he paid me back the money I lent him, and then we sort of drifted apart.

Limousines by Anthony was rolling on Pirelli tires, and then the infamous shitstorm arrived in 2008.

As Tony tells it:

> "There's this thing called the California Public Utilities
> Commission [CPUC]. One of their jobs is 'safety over-
> sight and enforcement of passenger cars.' You know how
> limousines have that TCP number on the back bumper?
> Well, that's from the CPUC. And I had those numbers,
> nice and legal. And then I get a call.

> "'Mr. Anthony Taylor, there's a bench warrant out for an
> Anthony Taylor from New York who has six kids and owes
> back child support for a few years, and that guy has your
> Social Security number, so come on down.'

> "I'm good, so I go down to straighten things out. I'm sure
> that I can explain. I'm not married and have no kids, so
> there must be a mistake.

> "I tell the guy that 45 years ago, when I was born, I was a
> 'left on the doorstep' kid and ended up being raised by my
> grandmother. She was old school, didn't know the rules,
> and when it came time to register me into kindergarten, I
> didn't have a birth certificate or anything, so the director
> of the school said that he would fill in the form for my
> grandmother with a 'retroactive Social Security number.' I
> know that makes no sense, but it was the 'hood, and that
> was how things went down there. And now here you are
> looking for an Anthony Taylor with six kids, but I've never
> been married and I don't have any kids.' It ain't me, babe,
> no, no, no, it ain't me."

Now you and I know that there's no such thing as a retroactive Social
Security number. You can get a replacement, but there's no category
called "retroactive." But I also know that the government makes mistakes
all the time, that Tony believes the story his grandmother told him,
and that Tony has no kids. So I'm pretty damn sure there's a mistake
and some explanation somewhere that could clarify everything. But

this misplaced and misunderstood Social Security number is about to get out of control.

Tony is told to report to the fraud department. He answers their questions, but they're still skeptical and ask if anyone can verify this tale. So Tony tells them to talk to his aunt Rudy and aunt Laura. They call the aunts, who confirm his story.

Tony said, "But they look at me and tell me they don't know who I am. They tell me I have to get a new birth certificate and a new Social Security number."

Well, proving a negative is impossible. Point of fact: the Anthony Taylor with the warrants is 5'10" and 175 pounds. Our Anthony Taylor is 6'3" and 255 pounds.

Tony hired a lawyer, but the wheels of justice grind slow, so while he's trying to prove that he legally exists, his assets are frozen, his bank account is debited $35,000, and the money is sent to Dorothy Taylor in New York City for her six kids, whom Big Tony has not fathered and has never met!

As crazy as it sounds, the PUC revokes his TCP license. He can't legally drive customers, so he can't pay his employees and can't pay the bank loans on his limousines. Tony goes broke and loses everything, except the one car that he ends up living in.

Tony said, "I served four years in the Marines, ran a business, and paid taxes for eight years, and here I was basically on earth as a nobody."

It took four years to clean up the mess. And it was about then that we reconnected, just as I was opening The Patio on Lamont restaurant. I heard Tony's story at the Cigar Lounge, and went and found him, and created a job for him—driving for me.

I leased him a car, made him a W-2 employee, and bought him a condo in Pacific Beach. He was my driver and "bodyguard." And then, of course, he ended up driving a lot of my other business associates around as well. He knew how to keep his mouth shut and his ears open.

Tony told me:

> "I've done a lot. I've been in the private airplanes and fancy
> hotel suites. I've been around. But I tell you, when I had
> your big shots in the back seat, I knew that all they saw
> was a big Black driver behind the wheel. I didn't really
> exist for them. They don't know me. I didn't trust them,
> and I thought they were just money grabbers.
>
> "You know, those people I grew up with in New York—
> they called me an overachiever. They all had parents and
> everything, but they didn't know me or my dreams, what I
> used to think about in my quiet times, what I was going to
> set out to do. I wasn't an overachiever; I never thought of
> myself as less than anybody. I was just an achiever. Period."

I confess that I'm quite fond of Big Tony, but I only believed about
75 percent of his story. However, I love creativity and the invention
of a "retroactive Social Security number." It fit in perfectly with my
invention of the "sister escrow," a term I fabricated (I'll explain more
about this later). Sure, you gotta do what you gotta do, but I'm not
proud of it.

It seems to me that one of the haunting issues in human nature is
the feeling of being underestimated or diminished—not being seen
for your true value or capabilities. It's what motivates many of us: the
twin desires of redemption and revenge, as in "I want to show those
bastards what I'm really worth."

Tony drove a lot of the promoters and bigger investors, and he was
asked by one of the attorneys if he thought those passengers ever
"knew." He said:

> "I think without a shadow of a doubt that Kim, Sider,
> Jai, Tom did—I mean, come on, man, it would take an
> idiot to not get it. Hell, I don't have a fancy degree, but
> I'm not dumb. Look, I employed people, I know how to

make money and get contracts, so if I could sit there and say that this math isn't adding up and this isn't right, you know what I mean? I wasn't eavesdropping, you understand, but man, it's right there."

***

When my program ended and the government took everything from me, Tony ended up homeless again, living in an SRO—an inexpensive single-room occupancy hotel room that rents by the week—with a bed, a small refrigerator, and a microwave. The world comes full circle again and again.

*** ***

CHAPTER 16
The Whistleblower

*"You know how to whistle, Steve, don't you, Steve? You just put your lips together and blow." —*Lauren Bacall's character in *To Have and Have Not*

I ntellectually, I knew that all Ponzi schemes come to an end at some point. But I had a vision that if I could bundle all my entities into one big basket and then take it public, before that point came I'd definitely be able to raise enough money to pay off all the investors, as well as give everyone a healthy return on their investments.

I needed time, and as long as people were getting their checks, no one was unhappy. There was no reason for anyone to put their lips together and do anything other than drink champagne and marvel at the profits.

But I knew that eventually someone would get their nose out of joint; someone would go poking around where they shouldn't poke, someone would want a better deal than anyone else had ever gotten (or at a minimum, want to understand the deal), and that's why real life mirrors the movies. Unfortunately, someone blew the whistle before I could cross the finish line.

In 2015, an investor friend of mine was approached to invest in a company called Aequitas, which had a home office in Lake Oswego, Oregon, but was active in San Diego. It was brought to him by a wealthy individual who was running the family office with a half billion in cash and assets. And the rich guy and my friend shared the same attorney, so that was how the connection was made.

This continues to support the underlying principle that the deal racket depends on knowing someone who knows someone you need to know. Aequitas was in the business of investing in portfolios of trade receivables in health care and education, among other areas. They would buy the "paper"—the debt the consumer owed to the institution—at a discount from hospitals and other organizations.

One organization they purchased receivables from was Corinthian Colleges, a collection of for-profit institutions of supposed higher learning. Corinthian recruited students whose tuition was funded by various government federal education funds, with the requirement and expectation that the students would repay the loans from the good jobs that their education would help them secure.

Aequitas bought the paper at a discount, and then they performed some kind of financial alchemy, packaged up the student debt, sprinkled holy water over it, and proceeded to solicit investors into their own program, promising returns in the midteens. This trick ranked right up there with turning coal into gold. The math made no sense to my friend. At least Penn and Teller tell you in advance that what you're seeing is all an illusion.

Ironically, two of the most active local promoters for Aequitas were members at the same Farms Golf Club that Kim and I belonged to. And that's how they found my friend, as usual on the first tee, with this deal that was unbeatable.

There's nothing like the first tee to warm people up to getting fleeced. "Nice to meet you, gorgeous day, what's your index. and how about a $20 Nassau, down 2, automatic press? Me, I haven't hit a ball in a year (and then he brings out a driver made in 1972). Tee it up." I don't know what it is about golf clubs that seems to attract practitioners of the art of the scam.

My pal reviewed the Aequitas offering material, and he couldn't understand their deal, so he called their mutual attorney, ready to confess his financial ignorance, but to his surprise, his attorney confessed that he couldn't understand how they made money either. So he passed, and so did his attorney.

The Aequitas program continued to raise millions until eventually it hit a large speed bump a couple years later. In May 2015, the for-profit Corinthian College program proved not only to have no profit, but also very little cash, and down they went in flames, filing for bankruptcy. When they did, Aequitas, which had lent Corinthian a large amount of money, was then stuck with a ton of worthless paper. But, unwilling to see the handwriting on the wall, Aequitas continued to raise money, not disclosing to the investors the truth about the bad loans to Corinthian and their inability to pay. So in March 2016, the SEC came calling on Aequitas, and the speed bump became a brick wall. Eventually they were forced to file for bankruptcy as well, having raised what the SEC claimed was "at least a $350 million Ponzi scheme, with new investor money largely going to pay off prior investors."

In an article for the *San Diego Reader*, Don Bauder, a financial journalist, wrote: "The story of Aequitas is one of colossal chutzpah and more likely colossal ignorance. Aequitas told investors the loans were safe because Corinthian vowed it would buy back any loans that were delinquent after 90 days."

They promised. Kim promised, and, unfortunately, I promised as well.

I take you to be my lawful wedded wife, promise to love you in sickness and in health, for richer or poorer, or at least as long as the prenup is still in effect. That's a promise.

Now Bauder was famous for exposing scams and cons. He was one of the best, but there was one guy even better than Bauder: a local financial fraud-watcher who saw the Aequitas debacle coming long before its final death rattle.

In March 2016, Bauder wrote: "Kevin Jasper, a San Diego lawyer, predicted that Aequitas would collapse, back in 2015, 17 months before it actually did. He said that the bad Corinthian loans would drain Aequitas of $70 million. I could not reach Jasper."

But Jasper was able to reach me. And I didn't know that he owned a whistle factory.

In the fall of 2018, I was introduced to Kevin Jasper by Tom Dobron, a wealthy investor in my program. Dobron lived in the Rancho Santa Fe area of San Diego, California. It's a community of big homes, fancy cars, trophy wives, and heaps of money. I liked Dobron, but I didn't completely trust him. He was relentless about getting his fees from bringing in investors.

In the past, he'd had some legal brush-ups with deals he'd done in Las Vegas, and there was also some litigation with City National Bank at one point.

Dobron was a wheeler-dealer with sharp elbows. He talked fast, was likable, and everybody loved him. He had the private jet, was doing real estate deals in Vegas, and was basically a man's man in the rough-and-tumble world of big-time homebuilding. He drank whiskey, played golf, and told dirty jokes—just the kind of guy I've had to work with or work around all my life. He reminded me of a character in the Tom Wolfe novel *A Man in Full*.

I was introduced to Dobron by Bruce Smith, who played ice hockey with my husband, Steve, and Smith was also a golfer who played with Dobron. As usual, it seemed that all roads ended up at the golf course. I think I would never have perpetrated this whole scam if I'd taken up tennis instead.

At any rate, Dobron, a guy who's always looking for a "get-rich-quick" scheme, comes to me and says he wants to go all in on the liquor-license program. The first question he asked me was about commissions: how much and when paid. And he wanted to understand how to get the money to Chicago. He had a foundation, Family First, and he intimated that the money was coming from offshore. I didn't press the issue. He invested that money and brought some of his friends along. I always wondered if his friends knew the commission deal.

Dobron had a friend of 25 years named Kevin Jasper. As you know, friends talk; they tell each other about the big, smart deals they're doing, so Dobron comes to me with a request. It was time for the secret handshake. I should have counted my fingers.

He wants me to meet his friend, who says he can put together a $50 million fund. Okay, and why did Dobron want to do this so badly? Easy: The commission deal with Jasper was going to be much richer than the one he had with me. He wanted to move from broker to principal.

Dobron sends me an email on September 5, 2018, saying:

> *Sorry to be a pest, as I know you are very busy. By coincidence one of my big investors is going to Saska's* [one of my most famous and successful restaurants], *on Friday night to celebrate the life of a mutual friend of ours that passed away last year unfortunately. He is the lawyer that I mentioned, named Kevin Jasper. Hope you can meet with him. Nice guy and very smart attorney. Told him that he will really love meeting you. Small world! Love ya, Tom.*

And this is why the world needs Google. Did it ever occur to me to look up Jasper? No, and I don't know why. I was always careful, but not this time. One of my favorite characters growing up was Nancy Drew. I loved those mysteries and had the entire collection. I read every book. She would have been more suspicious, but maybe I was just getting tired. I had my focus on the potential IPO. And if someone was claiming to be able to bring in that kind of money in one fell swoop, that was a meeting I was going to take. All I needed was to buy a little more time.

So I dressed up nicely and went to my restaurant. Dobron showed up, but no Jasper. I was a bit annoyed, but Dobron had his steak and martini, and I was out of there. And oh, by the way, Dobron never missed an opportunity: he asked me for the Padres box for the next home game.

Nothing came of the scheduled meeting, and the matter was off my radar for a few weeks. And then, again, suddenly, without warning, Dobron called, and with some urgency in his voice, wanted to set up a meeting right away, this time, at The Patio on Lamont. Three guys showed up: Tom Dobron, Kevin Jasper, and a third man (not to be confused with film villain Harry Lime), and we had the "meet." I don't remember the name of the third guy, unfortunately.

It was a short meeting, maybe 45 minutes total: no food, just drinks. It's funny how people make decisions and form opinions. You know, studies show that most of us make up our minds in the first 30 seconds of a discussion. Well, I didn't like Jasper. I couldn't pinpoint anything specific; I just didn't like him. And as for trusting him, well, he's a lawyer. Enough said.

After pleasantries were exchanged, Jasper and Dobron explained their plan to raise $50 million in a fund. But it was the third man who did a lot of the questioning. He asked how we could scale, about the rules in other states, and about licenses around the country, but there wasn't much discussion about how their deal would work with me, just some assurances from them that it was a done deal, going to happen, no problem. But I knew that the old 5 percent Dobron deal was long gone, girl. It was clear to me that Jasper didn't fool around for nickels.

In the end, Dobron said he'd roll his group of about $5 million into the bigger fund, and he and Jasper would be partners. But it seemed obvious to me that the only guy with any real money was the third man.

The meeting ended with assurances and handshakes, but I'd operated on my gut instincts in business for 25 years, so I wasn't comfortable. I had misgivings and rumblings, but this time, I didn't listen to them. I got blinded by the bullshit.

Oh, and Bruce Smith—he was never one to miss a trick. He wanted a spiff on Dobron and Jasper, so I had to agree to transfer my ownership in a condo in Palm Desert to him in lieu of ongoing commissions. Everyone had their hands out.

And then it was Christmas 2018. There were the usual bundler parties, so I made an appearance at Ilan's. I was on the no-fly list with Horacio, but mostly I ducked all of them. Steve and I were basically homebodies. A big night involved having a glass of wine and watching a movie. And then 2019 arrived—and with it, a new batch of 15 licenses.

After Kim got his first look, I sent the balance of the licenses to Dobron for him to do his picking, and then, unbeknownst to me, Dobron sent this list to Jasper for his review. Then Jasper did what no one else had done for almost seven years: some homework.

Jasper's analysis from the proposed list of licenses being presented for financing:

> Oakstone Winery, Inc.
>
> Price: $275,000
>
> Notes: Canceled license, but being reinstated by lawyer with partnership change/buyout/new financing, SBA loan, no property sale
>
> Location: Sacramento
>
> Expected COE (close of escrow) July 2019
>
> Return: 18%.

Jasper made a note in the margin that Oakstone was not a partnership, but rather, a corporation, and the license was canceled on February

19, 2013. Being called a partnership rather than a corporation may be considered a minor inconsistency, but Jasper went further. He checked the ABC site itself, and there in bold letters, it said: "A canceled license cannot be reactivated or reinstated."

Jasper made that note in the margin.

> Next one on the list:
>
> The Grand Avenue Café, Ltd.
>
> Price: $200,000
>
> Notes: On sale beer and wine, canceled, but being reinstated by lawyer through partnership buyout and new financing. SBA loan, No Property sale.
>
> Location: Oakland
>
> Expected COE: July 2019
>
> Return: 18%

Jasper did seem to be a stickler for details. He noted in the margin that it was not a partnership, but rather, was owned by an individual, Howie Le. The guy must have been a good lawyer. He liked details. So he kept digging and came up again with "A canceled license cannot be reactivated or reinstated."

> The Pizza Factory
>
> Price: $175,000
>
> Notes: On sale beer and wine, canceled but being reinstated through partnership buyout, relocation of license and new financing. SBA loan/No property sale.
>
> Location: Ontario
>
> Expected COE: July 2019
>
> Return: 18%

Another note in the margin: "License canceled, can't be reinstated."

I found out subsequently that Jasper sent an email and attachment to Dobron, as well as a few others, including Bruce Smith, on February 7, 2019. He'd reviewed the licenses being proposed for financing.

The subject line was telling: *These entries are bogus.* The email said:

> *I looked up the subject license numbers on the ABC license website for the transactions you picked to finance from the 1-19-2019 list. They all look suspect—all reinstating a canceled license via partnership buyout. Everything I've seen tells me a canceled license can't be reinstated.*
>
> *Some of these licenses were canceled 15 years ago. The most recent was canceled in 2015. All transactions are listed as partnership buyouts—only one licensee was a partnership (Lawrence Tam and Yong Yam)—and its license was canceled in 2004.*
>
> *This is getting crazier by the day and makes no sense. I'm baffled—but Gina keeps paying like clock-work* [sic].

When I saw that email, I did spend a minute on the clockwork line. I wasn't sleeping much at night and was in constant fear of being found out, of the whole thing collapsing around me in an avalanche before I could dig out and make everyone whole. Maybe I was just waiting for the knock on the door. Hell, all Jasper had to *do* was ring the bell.

But in February 2019, I didn't know anything. All I knew was that I never heard from Jasper again, and Dobron was suddenly not investing in any licenses. He'd gone stone-cold silent. And even more to the point, he began taking his money out of previous licenses, instead of his usual pattern of religiously rolling everything over and letting it ride. It was a sudden change of behavior, so I called call him to discuss.

Dobron gave me a song-and-dance about keeping his powder dry and how he was going to put his new money into the fund with Jasper. It sounded completely out of character for him to do so, as he always liked the action. When it came to red flags, maybe I should have been looking at my own flagpole.

In the meantime, licenses were waiting to be funded, so onward and upward; and other bundlers, like Kim, were bringing in dough hand over fist. The program logistics were enormous, and the complexity of all the moving pieces, the sheer volume of money flowing in and out, took all my attention. The Dobron anomaly didn't shout out loud enough to me at the time, but looking back, the handwriting was on the wall, and it was not a forgery.

So many of us look at life through a quartz prism, and the refractions and reflections can at times be misleading. I was busy running my businesses with almost 800 employees, and Jasper was busy doing his own forensic financial analysis. This guy was clearly in the dome car on the 3:10 to Yuma with the steam trumpet in his hand. I never saw the train coming.

But if he had suspicions, and if he had any intention of being a whistle-blower, hoping to get paid for information, he'd need to be more certain; he'd need to provide the SEC with "original information about a possible violation of the federal securities laws that has occurred or is ongoing." And I did not sell securities; I made loans. That was Kim's contention as well.

Jasper was an attorney, so he knew all the requirements for a potential false-claims-act lawsuit, and he developed a plan to do just that, to confirm the elements of the fraud. And Dobron delivered the ultimate Jasper fishhook: a Gamakatsu Round Bend treble baited with the detailed proposal for a $50 million fund in March 2019.

For years, Tom and I had worked our business arrangement almost exclusively by email. Sure, we got together from time to time, particularly when he was using the Padres box, but on this singular occasion, he brought the proposed-investment printed document in person. No email, no record, no trace. The document was a "Master Promissory Note" agreement for a structured fund to raise $50 million.

The document was thorough, detailed, and explained the various rights and obligations of the promoters—who gets what and when. It was a very professional piece of legal work, and I dug in to read it, closely and carefully. Sometimes I admit to being a deal-woman blasting along at 10,000 feet, but I'd gone to law school, and I knew that this document was not boilerplate and needed to be reviewed with caution.

Think about it: Jasper and I had one meeting, with him, Tom, and Mr. Third Man in the fall of 2018, and after the meeting, I never heard from him again. No slam bam, thank you, ma'am. Nothing. He never asked to meet Della or Bill Adams or Joelle or anyone. And then out of the blue in March 2019, I get this document for raising $50 million.

As I look back, maybe I'd read too many spy novels, but in retrospect, it was strange that it was Dobron who brought the document to me. Not Jasper and not by email. Okay, maybe FedEx was too expensive; maybe he wanted to just drop in and chat, but maybe I was being set up and simply didn't see it.

At that time, I didn't know about the email exchange between Jasper and Dobron in January and February, the exchange in which Jasper disclosed his findings that all the licenses being offered in the January package were expired or canceled.

Jasper's funding document was more rigorous and more detailed than any of the other agreements I'd entered into: no loopholes. When I read the document, I knew that this deal was never going to happen. It was Connelly and Grisham all bundled into one. I needed to walk away, and quickly.

The key feature of his deal was to require detailed documentation confirming a separate escrow for each license. That was not the way the program worked. There was so much money being sent to Chicago that I was being forced to "repurpose" some of the licenses. I was having to use old, expired, canceled, or nonexistent licenses to meet the demand, sometimes selling the same one multiple times. And there were never individual escrows. It was clear that Jasper and I were never going to reach a meeting of the minds.

I called him in April 2019 and said thank you, but it wasn't going to work for me. No details, just best wishes, and stay well. I only talked to Jasper twice—once to listen, and once to decline.

A month later, May 17, 2019, the subpoena from the SEC arrived.

I know there are coincidences in life, and someone always wins the lottery, but I'm laying down even money that Mr. Jasper still owns a whistle factory.

As for Tom Dobron, through his entities, he invested over $33 million and made slightly more than $1.7 million in fees.

*** ***

CHAPTER 17

The Feds Finally Figure It Out

Do not shred, spindle, or mutilate.

I n the movies, a man or woman over 18 years old comes to your door, knocks politely, hands you an envelope, and then says the magic words: "You've been served." Aghast or outraged, you quickly drop this burning-hot piece of paper on the floor and hope that since you've only touched it for a second, then perhaps you've avoided the service. Nope—not in the movies, and not in real life either. Even if the envelope is lying on the ground, you've been served! As a matter of fact, the U.S. Postal Service also appears to work quite well when it comes to sending services, and the SEC can use email. These are modern times, indeed. And more often than not, the service occurs when you're least expecting it.

Mine was delivered to the ANI offices in San Diego. It was a Friday, and I was at my vacation home in Carmel-by-the-Sea. Kim Peterson got his at his home in Del Mar. Subpoenas vary, but in this case, the key words were: "The staff of the Securities and Exchange Commission is conducting an investigation in the matter identified above."

Similar subpoenas were also sent at that time to my assistant, Joelle Hanson; and my controller, Cris Torres; and to Kim Peterson, Joe Cohen (one of the bundlers), and Tom Dobron and his son Nick (I think sending one to the son really pissed Tom off). And one subpoena in particular was sent to Chicago Title, requiring Della, Betty, and Tom to produce documents.

Subsequently, I learned that another dozen subpoenas were sent in the fall of 2020 through the spring of 2021 to other individuals of interest.

For those of you who've always walked the straight and narrow with comfortable shoes, herewith a short course on subpoenas from a non-lawyer: A subpoena is a writ issued by a government agency to compel testimony or produce evidence. In other words, it does not accuse you of a crime, nor does it come with custom handcuffs; rather, it indicates that you may be a person of potential interest (nothing personal, you understand; we just want a short chitchat with you).

At this point, the standard response is: "You must be kidding. There must be a mistake. Are you sure you have the right person?"

You can think of a subpoena as an invitation to a dinner party, date and location as indicated, and if it's not too much trouble, could you please bring your own silverware and don't worry about bringing the wine—just bring the documents. Oh, and one more thing: Do not under any circumstances shred any of those documents. The SEC uses the word *shred*—very old school, I think. The world lives on servers in the cloud today, and although the SEC doesn't specifically mention not wiping the hard drive, I think it's fair to say that this is their intention. The SEC seems to have a deep and abiding fascination with documents.

Kim helped me get an attorney, but he personally seemed extremely nonplussed. He assumed the issue was merely a technical violation of California lending laws since we weren't licensed financial brokers—that FINRA (Financial Industry Regulatory Authority) stuff. Kim had set up all his programs as loans, not as the sale of securities. At least that was his intention. He told me that the SEC was probably laboring under a "misunderstanding." Yeah, tell that to the judge.

I turned my legal-response work over to my attorney. People have asked me why I didn't just take $10 million, go to Vietnam or Indonesia or some other country with no extradition treaty, and do a Marc Rich (the fugitive international financier). Never. It wasn't in my DNA to disappear. The thought never crossed my mind. After all, I'm a deal lady, and I needed to get back to running the businesses and taking care of Steve. I didn't show overt concern over the subpoenas to my team, but in my gut, I knew it was serious and, again, in retrospect, maybe I was kind of relieved that the end was in sight.

And then in June, as if to poke the SEC in the eye, in an act of defiance right after getting the subpoena, I gave first-class plane tickets to Della to go to Cabo San Lucas for some well-deserved rest and recreation. I was dancing with the devil, and I was waiting for the music to end.

***

I'd had a long relationship with Kim Peterson. All in, he probably accounted for more than $110 million put into the program. But Kim's suggestion that the SEC had a "misunderstanding" was ludicrous. That ranks with a belief in UFOs or aliens landing in Times Square.

"I'm sure it was just a misunderstanding, Officer. I know I was going 110 in a 35-mile-per-hour zone, but I had both hands on the wheel, and my cell phone was in the glove compartment along with my unregistered .44 Magnum."

After the subpoenas arrived, Kim met with me. We had coffee, and he wondered aloud that maybe the SEC was confused and thought it was money laundering or a Ponzi scheme. I nearly did the classic "spit-take." But then I replied calmly, "Yeah, I think you're right. Probably just some confusion about the sale of securities and our loan program."

I assured him that he was still going to get his fees, and in the end, that's all he was really concerned about. Kim was still blind and in deep denial.

Kim, you've just stepped off the subway platform and are about to touch the third rail. In one sentence, you've used the two magic words, *laundering* and *Ponzi*, which are the equivalents of having a plastic explosive strapped to your nuts, with the detonator in the hands of the government.

My advice to Kim at that coffee meeting was to get the best lawyer he could and to stop passing GO and collecting $200. Deaf ears. Between May 2019 and August 31, 2019, Kim personally raised $13 million for the liquor-license program. Other bundlers and investors poured in another $7 million. That $20 million over those three months was astonishing, given that the subpoenas were hiding in plain sight.

And what about Chicago Title? They also got the subpoena at the same time. It came in the mail, apparently ended up on someone's desk, and strangely, nobody said nothing to nobody. A subpoena arrived and it ended up in the dead-letter file? Really?!

With all due respect, did it occur to you guys, at any time after receiving a subpoena on this program, to say something to anyone, to alert any executive, to wander down and have a chat with Della and her girls, maybe give me a call and ask me what was up? Or did you consider it more like an offer from AT&T to bring high-speed fiber to your building or make it into a paper airplane?

It was business as usual at Chicago until that day in August 2019 when I threw in the towel, met with the SEC, and filed a guilty plea. Greed is one powerful motherfucking emotion, ain't it? Everyone seemed prepared to go down swinging. They shoot horses, don't they? Just keep dancing.

At least I was willing to look at the inevitable and see that a small cell was going to be my condo for a few years.

But after receiving the subpoena in May, I got scared. I did what guilty people do: I stopped thinking clearly and made a massively stupid mistake. I began to shred documents and tried to hide things. The Feds have taken advanced courses in finding out where you hide things. They have a PhD in looking through your underwear drawer, ignoring the lace thongs, and picking up the shredded email stack and gluing it back together. I took boxes of stuff to a vacation rental I owned. Then the SEC went there and found them. The idea that the Feds would think to go to a vacation rental—can you imagine that? Ha!

This was insanity, and I paid for it with the added criminal count of "obstructing justice." I knew it was over, and I wanted it over, but at the same time, like so many of us when cornered, I figured maybe there was one more offramp on the freeway and I could escape in a white Bronco. When the government knocks at your door, trust me, most of us will just shit our pants.

I was afraid but not terrified. I was in that calm place where reality seems to slow down, you see things clearly, and although I was ready to fold my cards, I was also still holding on to the wild idea that I could get the IPO done and pay everyone back.

*** ***

CHAPTER 18

The Plea Agreement

If we make a deal, will you keep your word?

I confessed. And that's how a plea agreement works.

On August 27, 2019, Big Tony drove me up to the Los Angeles office of the SEC, where my attorneys and I met with officials for four hours.

At that meeting, the SEC made it clear that they had enough evidence to charge me with "securities fraud, in violation of 15 U.S.C. 77q and 77x; obstruction of justice, in violation of 18 U.S.C. 1505; and conspiracy to commit securities fraud and obstruct justice, in violation of 18 U.S.C. 371."

Further, "Defendant agrees to waive indictment and plead guilty . . . in exchange the Government agrees not to bring additional charges. . . ." And the whole agreement rests precariously and precisely on my not "breaching the plea agreement or the guilty plea."

For those of you who like all the details, here are the three charges in the plea agreement:

> **Securities fraud:** Defendant willfully used a scheme
> to defraud someone, or obtained money or property by

someone by means of an untrue statement or omission of material fact; Defendant's acts were undertaken, and her statements were made, in the offer or sale of one or more securities; and Defendant directly or indirectly used the instruments of interstate commerce in connection with undertaking these acts and making these statements.

Obstruction of Justice: Defendant knew that a proceeding was pending before the United States Securities Commission; and Defendant corruptly endeavored to influence obstruct or impede the due and proper administration of the law under which the proceeding before the United States Securities and Exchange Commission was being conducted.

Conspiracy: There was an agreement among two or more persons to commit offenses, to wit, securities fraud and obstruction of justice. The defendant became a member of the conspiracy knowing of at least one of its objects and intending to help accomplish it, and one of the members of the conspiracy performed at least one covert act for the purpose of carrying out the conspiracy.

While there might be nuances as to the definition of *securities fraud* and ultimately whether it was me or the bundlers or Chicago Title or other co-conspirators who could, at some later date, as more information came out, additionally fall under the SEC jurisdiction, for then I was okay to leave that to some other high-priced pencil necks in the future.

I'm a fan of the card game "Hearts," and my assessment was that I'd pulled the Black Queen, and no discards were left. You have to play the cards you're dealt.

The suits always get the last word: "Defendant has fully discussed the facts of this case and defendant has committed each element of the crime and admits there is a factual basis for this guilty plea."

Yup.

But the reason why I agreed to take the fall early and plead guilty is because there was an implied understanding, if not a firm deal, that certain things would happen, to my benefit, as long as I cooperated and assisted in their discovery, understanding, and recovery of assets. In other words, I was relying on the SEC, and eventually the U.S. Attorney's Office as well, to keep their end of the bargain. And for sure, I was fully determined to do everything I could to assist in their efforts to recover all monies for the investors.

But a triangle has three sides, and the unknown hypotenuse is the judge. On that subject, it often comes down to luck of the draw.

For those of you who've never been in a situation like this, to fully understand the finality of pleading guilty, I assure you the initial instinct is always to plead "Not guilty."

Even when your hand is literally stuck in the cookie jar, you always figure you might get lucky, maybe the jar is defective, maybe the jury will OD on chocolate chips, and you could always live to fight another day. Except when you don't.

In the world of negotiation and dealmaking, there's a concept called BATNA, which stands for Best Alternative to a Negotiated Agreement. In other words, if they have you dead to rights and there's no way out, then you make the best deal you can at the time with the facts and cards you have. And that's what I did.

I agreed to fully cooperate—to explain and reveal and implicate. It was a complicated scheme, and it took a lot of people participating, either through active involvement or just looking the other way, to pull it off. I mean, $400 million may not be in the same league as Bernie Madoff, but this was still the largest Ponzi scheme ever run by a woman acting alone in America.

One of the threads that runs through my story is that of being a woman in a man's world. I'm not an apologist; there's no excuse for what I did, but for the 50 percent of the country that's female, there are some realities that the other half simply cannot fully, intellectually, or in their gut, understand. Men can pay lip service, they can be informed, they can be enlightened, they can promote and encourage and honor women as a gender, but deep down, hardcore, I know, and so do you, that it's different for women. Just plain, fucking different.

***

Big Tony drove me back home from Los Angeles that afternoon in August. We rode in silence for most of the trip. When I met him, he was living in his car. I gave him a job, took care of him, got him a place to live. I looked at him in the rearview mirror, and he showed no fear, but I knew that he knew that he would be on his own again very soon and might very well end up living in his car again.

I reread the plea agreement in the car, and there was one sentence that did make me smile: "The Defendant accepted responsibility when first approached by criminal authorities . . . and has saved resources the Government would otherwise have spent prosecuting the case."

I've always been an inveterate optimist. I can always find the bright light, even at midnight during a power failure. But I was glad it was over. I was relieved. Sure, I wish that I'd had the courage to stop sooner, but I was caught in the maelstrom that I'd created, and the waters were just too damn deep.

I knew that I was going to disappoint a lot of people—a *lot*. I'd agreed in that meeting to go in with the SEC jointly to request a receivership to take over all my assets, all the businesses, and that I would essentially be locked out of them without any further activity. Maybe I could have fought, but I went in for full cooperation. It was the right thing to do because I wanted to help my victims. I always believed that I was going to somehow get that money back to them and continue to make them a lot of money in the end, when they were all paid out.

It's difficult to give up certain beliefs that keep a person attached to this earth. They start out cast in concrete, and I truly believed, given enough time, that I could and would make it right and make everyone whole. It sounds delusional when I say it now, but at the time, I needed to believe that there was light at the end of the tunnel and that everyone would live happily ever after. I knew then that the concrete had cracked.

In the car that afternoon, I questioned whether I'd been running toward a dream or running as fast as I could from the disappointments and failures of my past.

My biggest fear was for my husband, my family, my friends, and the shock and anger that I knew was coming. I'd just been appointed a trustee at the University of San Diego, something I'd worked hard for, so I got on the phone the next day, called the monsignor, and resigned. Before anything hit the paper, I wanted to prevent him from enduring any embarrassment.

I wanted to call people and apologize directly, to express my regret and remorse, but given the terms of the plea agreement, I was forbidden from contacting the investors. Apparently, it could be construed as witness tampering. It's a lonely place when you want to atone, and there's nobody around to listen.

Some friends stayed by my side, and others shunned me like a leper. You never know. I was always amazed, because you think you know the ones who'll stick by you, and you're wrong. But then some people you never really knew come out of the woodwork, call you, and wish you well. That was a very pleasant surprise.

But in the end, I don't really trust people. I just think it's human nature that everybody is self-absorbed and out for themselves, for the most part. I guess I have a cynical view of human beings. My favorite quote is from Mark Twain: "The more I learn about people, the more I like my dog."

***

After Big Tony drove me back from the SEC meeting in LA, I went home, changed my clothes, and went to the Farms Golf Club, where the Ladies Team Play was having its annual dinner. I was a member of the team and didn't want to let them down. But I did take a few of my closest friends aside to tell them what was going to be happening in the newspaper over the next couple days. I wasn't disappointed. My girlfriends were very supportive—all but one—who basically called me a couple of four-letter words.

Most of those in my world were supportive. That doesn't mean they thought I was innocent. There was never any question about the crime. Rather, what that means is they tried to be understanding, they tried to be sounding boards, they tried to be helpful to Steve.

But the real challenge for me was to look inside and find a truth I could hold on to.

The day after I got back from Los Angeles, I went into the corporate office and let my direct reports know what was about to come down. We then held meetings with *their* direct reports. I met with my legal advisers, who weren't involved with the case, to inform them about was happening. We made a companywide announcement that a receiver would be appointed as soon as the judge approved the joint stipulation that the SEC and I had agreed to.

When the receiver, Krista Freitag, was appointed, she brought her team into our office. They took over our conference room, and I met with them for two days. I walked them through all the businesses, brought in the department leaders so they could explain *their* respective businesses, and also brought in investors in other businesses in which I was involved. It was a massive download exercise, and I was exhausted, both physically and emotionally.

At the end of the download sessions, the receiver decided to close every business and real estate development deal with the exception of four businesses and the vacation rentals, which would honor preexisting bookings. She fired all of our corporate employees except for the human resources director, her assistant, and a few others. The businesses she kept open included The Patio on Lamont, Surf Rider Pizza in La Mesa and Ocean Beach, and Saska's restaurant in Mission Beach.

*** ***

CHAPTER 19
The Jig Is Up
"Just the facts, ma'am." —the Joe Friday
character from *Dragnet*

The word *jig* comes from a lively dance popular in the Elizabethan era, and thus the phrase "The jig's up, Betty, both hands in the air" is that moment when you look at your partner and realize that you're going to see less of him for the next few years, because visiting privileges are limited in prison.

That evening I was going to have to do some serious explaining to my husband, Steve, who knew nothing about nothing for all these years.

But there were still more people to meet. It turns out that a confession is more than just a quick chat with the priest, a few Hail Marys, and you're good to go. Not so fast. After the SEC, there were some other folks who wanted to discuss my future.

On September 18, 2019, my lawyers and I met with several gentlemen and one woman from the U.S. Attorney's Office (two of them), the SEC (two of them), and the FBI (one was more than enough) in the SEC office in San Diego. I'd witnessed this scene many times on TV, but when it's you, yourself, sitting in that windowless conference room downtown, it becomes a bit more daunting and indelible.

They started by giving me the speech—you know, the one where they explain how bad it could be if you don't tell the truth.

Drew, the lead SEC lawyer, was very nice. He didn't launch into a fire-and-brimstone, scare-me-to-death tirade. He just asked me politely to not lie to them, because they would find it all out anyway, and then it would be worse. Good by me. I was ready to give it up.

They offered me the "Queen for a Day" treatment (what is technically known as a proffer agreement). A *proffer* is a legal term that stipulates that anything you say in this particular process will not be held against you in a future criminal proceeding. It provides a supposed assurance that you can tell the truth to the government. I said no to that offer; I told them I was all in and ready to talk on the record, with full cooperation.

The meeting lasted four hours, and I laid out the program from inception right up until that moment in that room. One moment at this meeting struck me as odd. Normally, the Feds don't volunteer much information, but I was surprised when the other SEC gentleman said, "It does seem suspicious to us that Tom started taking his money out this year." I straightened up in my chair. I suddenly knew where that comment came from, even if my lawyers didn't.

Remember, it was January of 2018 when Kevin Jasper wrote to Tom Dobron to tell him that the list of licenses he was looking at was "bogus." And it was in February when I'd noticed that Dobron wasn't rolling his dough over like always. And it was in March when Dobron approached me with Jasper's proposal, the bait, which I'd rejected. And then it was in May when I got the subpoena, and now in September 2019, like the tumbler on a safe, all the pieces clicked together, and the vault door sprang open. The Feds had the playbook: *Follow the money*.

Dobron got his own subpoena for his records on March 10, 2021. No good deed goes unpunished, and the wheels of justice grind slow, but they grind fine.

Over the next 30 days, I had five more four-hour meetings with the same cast of characters. The Feds were very polite and respectful. It took them a long time to really understand how the whole thing worked. I named names that they didn't know, and that went a long way in helping them understand the other parties who should be prosecuted.

My exit strategy had been to do a public stock offering that would include my entire portfolio of businesses and restaurants, with their management contracts and retail and clothing and coffee—essentially the whole "Gina"—and then repay everyone with the proceeds. I'd met with investment bankers who were considering the idea when it all ended. But that idea wasn't grounded in any reality, because any half-witted investment banker who started real due diligence would quickly see that the money behind all these businesses didn't really belong to me.

The money I took from Chicago was used to support the "Gina Empire." I had "borrowed" it without agreement from other people who thought they were loaning on liquor licenses, not investing in restaurants and retail businesses. Over the previous seven years, I'd used about $60 million of the money for myself and for my various businesses, according to the plea agreement, although I think it was less. I had almost 800 employees—that's a lot of payroll. I was running the empire I wanted, but it required cash to keep it afloat. But many of the businesses *weren't* profitable, and I needed cash to prop them up. So I used the liquor-license loan funds to make payroll and do new acquisitions.

I lived a compartmentalized life. Some people saw me as cold and calculating; others saw me as generous and caring. What *I* saw depended on which mirror I looked in. But I knew it was a crime. People have asked me, "If you knew it was a crime, why did you do it?" Well, I'll be writing "letters from prison" for a more few years now, and I think I'll have more than enough time to figure that out.

The most memorable part of that day in September was when Drew, the younger U.S. Attorney, walked me to the elevator. He took my hand to shake it, pulled me a little bit closer to him, and said, "I've always wanted to meet you. I respected your previous civic work in San Diego, and I just wish it were under different circumstances." He turned and walked away, and I pushed the down button on the elevator and left.

*** ***

CHAPTER 20

The Five Stages of Investor Grief

"And that's the way it is." —Walter Cronkite

I
magine opening up the local paper, the *San Diego Union-Tribune*, and there on the front page is a story—the essence of which is that you probably have less money on that morning than you had the day before.

Investors called me, and I took every call. I never ducked a single one. And investors called Chicago Title as well. I don't know how they responded.

Dr. Elisabeth Kübler-Ross developed a model for dealing with grief. She formulated the various stages as a guide for terminal-illness patients and their loved ones as they try to come to terms with impending death.

Although in most cases, losing money doesn't have the same life-and-death impact as a malignant glioblastoma (or any of the other untreatable diseases that ravage humankind), nonetheless, some of my investors thought they were quite similar.

If you'll allow me a bit of schadenfreude and dark humor, here is the range of investor responses upon learning that approximately $153 million of their money, at that time, was unaccounted for.

Denial

"There must be a misprint. What do you mean there's only $11 million at Chicago Title? There's supposed to be about $120 million in the escrow account. I need to call those damn women at Chicago Title and get to the bottom of this incredible screw-up. This cannot be right; there must be a mistake. I have the paperwork in front of me. It says that my money is safe in an escrow. What's the phone number at the title company? I need to call immediately. This is obviously only a clerical error. Ridiculous."

Anger

Initially directed at the bundler who brought them into the deal, it then morphs into a general rant delivered standing in the street in front of the title company or the office or the house of the guy who knew the guy you needed to know, who got you into this piece of shit.

"You motherfuckers! What do you mean there's no money? Where's my fucking money? I'm going to sue every one of you cocksuckers. What do you think, I'm just going to roll over and play dumb? You haven't heard the last of me. You'll hear from my lawyer. Where the fuck is my money? You put me into this piece of shit, you get me out of it. I want my money!"

Bargaining

Now it's time for the lawyers. So far, 11 lawsuits had been filed (for sure, some will be settled by the time of this book's publication), all claiming and naming, in various configurations, everyone who was ever a John Doe or knew a Doe or who ever bought a drink in a restaurant that had a liquor license that was secured by a loan from any one of the 280 investors in the liquor-license Ponzi scheme.

And, of course, the obvious place where lawyers go to look for that money is in the "deep pockets" of someone who wears pants that have pockets. Hello, Chicago Title Insurance Company, meet the tailer who sews pockets. Chicago is owned by Fidelity National Title Group, #523 on the Fortune 1000, with a current market cap of about $11 billion. This company has a closet full of pockets.

Depression

This expresses itself in a variety of ways, from coming home and kicking the cat to taking a gun and biting the bullet (literally). No one did that. For a further exploration of depression, you should consult the *Diagnostic and Statistical Manual of Mental Disorders, DSM-5.*

Depression is a broad emotion, but the baseline starting position often morphs into self-flagellation: "How could I be so dumb? I should have known better, but how could I have known, after all? Manny was in the deal, and Manny has a big house and the Lambo, and I've always admired Manny and his smarts—you know, he's a very smart guy."

And, "Look, I know, I know, it's all my fault. But, Jesus Christ, how could this happen to me? This is a disaster. I'll never be able to look at my children again [you may substitute *wife* here if she hasn't already divorced you for this stupidity, after she told you more than once that it was a dumb idea and what the hell did you know about liquor licenses, other than the fact that you drink too much, and we haven't had sex in three years].

And, "Their inheritance is gone. I was never a good parent, and the only way I could have ever hoped to redeem myself was to leave them a lot of money so that when I'm dead, they'll have some kind thoughts, but now that I can't leave them the money, they'll hate me, and I hate myself as well."

And, "I wonder if my life insurance is paid up. I saw a movie where the guy hooks a hose up to the tailpipe, but I own a fucking electric car, and that's never going to work."

But still, always in the quiet of the night, looking into the fireplace, alone with a glass of whiskey [Johnnie Walker Blue Label—look, he lost a lot of money, but he's not gonna drink swill under any circumstances], there's the plaintive lament: *Wherethefuckismymoney?*

Acceptance

And sometimes acceptance leads to forgiveness. I'm always astounded, and moved almost to tears, when the woman stands up in the crowded courtroom, at the final sentencing, during those moments when the victim gets one last chance to speak to the person who ruined her life, killed her son, raped her daughter, or whatever, and standing in front of the evildoer (admittedly on his way to prison for 300 years plus two life terms without parole), she looks directly into his eyes and says, "I forgive you. I pray for your soul." That is the power of grace and forgiveness. It is something to aspire to.

I met for 25 minutes on Zoom with the probation officer who would write the "Pre-sentence Investigation Report." These are the counts to which I pled guilty:

Count One: Conspiracy, a Class D felony

Count Two: Securities Fraud, a Class D felony

Count Three: Obstruction of Justice, a Class D felony

The maximum for each count was five years, and the probation report multiplied it by three, so the maximum was 15 years. Easy math— anyone can do it. Add them up, don't divide by anything, and you come up with 15.

In the biblical search for justice and mercy, the report has a section called "Victim Impact." It includes letters from people who attest to my good character, and also letters from outraged investors.

Here's a sample of what people wrote (the comments in parentheses are mine):

#1: "I feel Gina did this to me personally, I do not have enough money to live on, I have lost faith in people and I can't trust anyone. Please give her the max you can by law."

(The stated loss for this investor was $150,000. As a point of fact, I'd never met or spoken with this aggrieved investor. The money was just wired to Chicago Title, and this investor got into the deal from the bundler running the California Opportunity Fund, LLC.)

#2: "I cannot trust anyone. She wanted to hurt us personally. Please give Gina the max. It is not only money!! It is our trust in others."

(If not being able to trust your fellow human beings is an event that qualifies for monetary recovery, be sure to send your request to the U.S. Congress and the U.S. Senate, and don't forget to copy your local city officials. Her loss was $150,000.)

#3: This victim reported a loss of $100,000. The loss has caused her "considerable duress."

(I'll tell you that traffic on the damn I-5 South at 5:00 p.m. causes me considerable duress also, so I get her vibe. But she goes on.)

#3 (cont'd.): "The way this investment was presented to me it was a safe no loss, win-win situation with a high percentage return. It was personally guaranteed by Gina Champion-Cain. Obviously, this meant absolutely nothing."

(She claims to suffer from depression and a nervous breakdown. And she claims her parents invested as well and lost money. Her investment was $50,000. Without being unkind, it's one thing for you to take a flyer, but bringing your parents into this crazy scheme may qualify as elder abuse. It just means less of an inheritance.)

#4: This victim says that her father suffered a heart attack when he found out that he had lost everything. This whole thing has "taken a huge toll on our family." The father's total investment was $150,000.

(I do not minimize anyone's financial loss, but if your father has "lost everything," then he was certainly not an accredited investor and had no business doing this deal. Call your bundler. I've never spoken to this person.)

#4 (cont'd.): "I pray she gets the MAXIMUM sentence the law can give her."

Here's a sample of what others wrote about me in a more positive light—a view from the home team:

— "She is deeply remorseful and has expressed this to me multiple times. She has never tried to excuse or justify what she did. I have seen her acts of kindness. I know she will commit the rest of her professional life to repairing the harm she has admitted to causing."

— "I have known Gina to be a good person for more than three decades. I have seen her take care of her employees during hard times, paid legal bills for someone getting divorced, mentored young women starting businesses. You can usually tell a good person if she has a dog who loves her. Gina has four."

— My priest: "I have known her as a good person, she has been a trustee here. She has done charitable and community work throughout the region. I am sure she will use these times and her mistakes to become better and help others to learn from her actions."

(But on balance, I will admit that the scales were definitely tilted in the other direction. Back to being burned at the stake.)

#5: "This scam could not have happened without Chicago Title. I feel betrayed by a very close friend (not Gina), this was a heartless crime of greed."

His stated loss was $550,000, "plus 25 percent for my contingency lawyer." On the matter of greed, the ruling on the field stands.

And finally, this one, in writing, for the judge and all the world to see:

#6: Victim had a "reported loss of $1,365,000." His further opinion is that "defendant is a parasite and a lying sack of shit. If this were under ancient biblical law, defendant should have her hands cut off."

(I think he's referring to Hammurabi's Code.)

Look, I've confessed to the crime, and I feel only shame and remorse, but a lawyer friend of mine took the position that each investor must bear what he calls some degree of "negligent culpability"—recklessly acting without reasonable caution, carelessness, and not being aware of a substantial and unjustifiable risk.

I guess that's why the world created lawyers.

*** ***

CHAPTER 21

Some Investors Choose Mediation

"I made all my money by selling too soon."
—Bernard Baruch

I know that Shakespeare suggested some appropriate thoughts about lawyers in *Henry VI*: "Let's kill all the lawyers." But the truth is that they're often the refuge of last resort when you're looking to find a way out of a mess.

And so it was time for the legal eagles to step to the forefront. There were multiple groups of unhappy investors, and they hired multiple groups of lawyers. In all, at the beginning, there were more than a dozen lawsuits filed against Chicago, Kim Peterson, and others, but never against me personally. I'd thrown in the towel to the SEC, the U.S. Attorney, and the receiver, and my goal was to explain in extreme detail how the Ponzi scheme worked, who benefited, and where all the skeletons were buried. I was all in on trying to help recover as much money as possible.

But one thing about lawyers—including those working for the receiver, as well as the receiver herself—everyone wants to get in on the assault, and for sure, every one of them wants to get paid. Some by the hour, some on contingency, some in a hybrid form, but nobody's doing nothing without some expectation of remuneration. They all expressed their deep concern to the investors, and their firm desire to assist in the recovery, but in the end, there's always the matter of their fees.

The basic legal theory was to go after the deepest pockets, and those belonged to Chicago Title.

What I found fascinating was this: I read every single lawsuit, front to back, cover to cover. More or less, they all said the same thing. It was as if one lawyer group simply took the other guy's work, changed the first page, and then made photocopies of the document. It's a personal matter here, but if I were an investor, I'd like to get back as much money as I could, without paying the legal community to rinse and repeat each time.

After cycling through Denial and Anger, the investor groups come to Bargaining, and this is where the lawyers came in. It was time to consider the various options. Some of the investors weren't part of a formal "fund"; they invested on their own, or through a bundler, but now was the time to find strength in numbers, and even though you might not really know the other investors, like being in a lifeboat where you don't get to pick your seatmate, still, you're there because you're now linked by a common goal: "Is there *any* way to get my money back?"

This is classic stuff, like being stranded on a mountain; or my favorite story of all: Ernest Shackleton and his ship, *Endurance*, trapped in the ice for ten months before it sank. Then Shackleton kept his men together for two years, leading them all to safety on Elephant Island. He did not lose a single man. They don't make them like Shackleton anymore. By the way, without being snotty, I don't think there were any lawyers on the *Endurance*.

But there was an early group who saw the writing on the wall. They got organized, and they made some really good decisions. The first being, they hired a very smart attorney; and second, they did *not* file a lawsuit. They were going to try mediation. You know, that's what the lawyers tell you to do at the beginning of your divorce, before you go ballistic and end up burning your own house down.

Their plan was led by a very small group of three investors who started by looking to sign up a larger pool of investors in order to create scale for their effort. They signed up 47 aggrieved investors. Some jumped on the bandwagon eagerly, and some needed to be pushed a bit, but in the end, they had a group with enough similarities and shared goals. But 47 was too many people to be effective, so now they had to slim it down, so they formed an executive committee. Democracy in action: one person, one vote. The executive committee ended up with seven members.

It was still too big, though, so they winnowed that committee down to a "steering committee" of three, but all 47 got to vote. Winning the steering-committee election was like running for high school student-body president, because more than a few of the investors saw themselves as savvy and sophisticated dealmakers of substance, and even felt that perhaps there should have been a recount at the executive-committee level. You can draw your own conclusions as to ego and arrogance at a later time.

When the ballots were counted (and recounted), three men were elected to the steering committee: one smart, wealthy fellow from New York; one aggregator; and one smaller investor who just happened to be an attorney. He wasn't a corporate-deal guy or a litigator, but rather a professional mediator, someone who resolves issues rather than hiring the local flame-thrower company. This was a fortuitous turn of events for this group. Let's call this mediator "Jones."

The next step for the steering committee was to develop a strategy and get buy-in from the rest of the group. If all 47 investors in this group got to talk, nothing good would happen, and everyone would probably freeze to death. And to compound the puzzle, this group of investors ranged in net worth from $300,000 or so to more than $30 million. So, for some, the loss was significant, and for others, they wouldn't have to worry about missing a meal.

Jones explained that if you wanted to be part of the group and get the benefit of fee sharing and so on, you had to agree to be bound by the final decision of the members of the executive committee. There were a couple of meetings of the 47 where everyone could ask questions, and it was clear that some people wanted blood, other people just wanted out, other people understood the risk, and others believed that this was going to be a huge windfall. And almost all of the investors in this group thought highly of their own investment skills.

Jones told a friend of mine at the very end that his hardest job was to get the investors to acknowledge that they might have played a role themselves in their decision-making. They needed to come to personal grips with the fact that it was unlikely that any court would find Chicago Title 100 percent liable for their losses.

The "Jones Group" had a claimed "net loss" of about $23 million. The concept of net loss proved to be important. In any Ponzi scheme, it's possible for some investors who've been in the program a long time to get back multiples of their original investment, and other investors who came late to the party to get nothing. The net loss for this discussion is the total you put in minus the total you got back, without regard to "profit" or "interest" payments. You don't get to count those, and you may not get to keep them either. The concept of net loss will come into play in the later receiver litigation, when the "clawback" dragon rears its ugly head in an effort to recover any "ill-gotten gains." But I'm getting ahead of myself.

So, the next problem for Jones was to pick an attorney to represent the group in the mediation. This was a critical step, and Jonesy got it 100 percent right. He hired William Calderelli, a very experienced litigator, and then the group made another good decision: no contingency; they would pay the hourly rate. Sure, some of the investors questioned if they were throwing good money after bad, but the steering committee held firm, and the group stayed together on that decision. Think about shared goals and the possibility of unintended consequences on that one.

This was not as easy a decision as you might think. At first blush, if the attorney was going to work on contingency, that might appear to be the obvious choice—no more money out of your pocket. But let's do some math together. If the ultimate settlement from Chicago is $100, and your "net loss" was $150, and then you deduct the 35 percent legal contingency fee, your net recovery is $65, which is a 43 percent recovery on your lost money.

So then you have to do some more math. How much are the legal fees if we just pay and don't do contingency? And where is the crossover point when it's better to pay hourly? And then the double straddle: Are the best interests of the parties more aligned or less aligned if the plaintiffs are paying hourly, and is it more or less likely that a settlement will occur sooner or later?

Enter COVID. Suing was certainly an option, but when would they get into court? The federal court system was backed up, and the unknowns were large.

You can see that you might not really have wanted to be on that steering committee.

Calderelli made the decision for the group. He wasn't a contingency lawyer, so they were now in for hourly. Okay, the next obvious dilemma to resolve: they needed some money for legal fees, and who was going to chip in?

Jones wanted everyone to have some skin in the game, but some people had more skin than others. Their strategy was to raise enough money to poke the bear and see if they could win in mediation, and if they couldn't, then raise a large pot of money and join the other lawyers suing Chicago Title.

Damn clever. Normally you sue the bastards to get their attention, and then you say let's get together and discuss settling. Offering the olive branch before the poison ivy was unique and ultimately proved to be the most cost effective.

Agreeing to contribute some pro rata legal fees was one thing, but agreeing to a final settlement for some number was quite another. If your loss was 1 percent of your net worth, your interest in, and input into, the mediation might well be different than if your net-worth loss was 25 percent. But, of course, human beings aren't rational, and some of the 1 percent guys were the loudest and most determined. Some people just wanted their day in court. They'd seen too many Perry Mason episodes.

So Chicago Title picked Steve Strauss as their attorney, who was, without question, one of the top guys in San Diego and maybe beyond. But Jones had to temper expectations. This was not a slam-dunk case.

However, there was a wrinkle in the mediation. Remember when I was sensing some red flags in the program, I decided to open a new bank account at Chase Bank in the name of "Chicago Escrow and T," and about a half dozen of the investors in their group of 47 had wired their money to that account—not to the real Chicago Title? So, not only were they in a Ponzi scheme, but they hadn't even wired the money to the right bank. There were no fake escrows at Chase Bank; there were no escrows at all! And now this group wanted Chicago to make them whole as well, along with the others.

The last critical decision for Jones was choosing a mediator. Jones let Chicago make the pick. Like winning the toss and electing to receive. That turned out to be brilliant, since the guy they picked, Layn Phillips, was the one of the most effective and most respected (and also most expensive) guys in the mediation business in Southern California. Remember, it was their pick, so Jones was buying some goodwill right off the bat by agreeing to this fellow. Phillips was old school; he showed up with nothing more than a blue pen and a yellow pad.

There were ten hours of negotiating. Right out of the movies, where the mediator went to Chicago in one room and said, "I'm not saying that Jones would say yes to this number, but if they said yes to that number, would you consider saying yes?"

And then Phillips went to the Jones Group and said that Chicago wasn't agreeing to this number, but if they did agree to the number, would *you* agree to the number?"

Finally, both sides got to the end of the day. Every deal guy knows that you need a deadline; it's a classic Japanese negotiation technique. And they'd only paid for Phillips until 7:00 p.m. The clock was ticking.

Finally, at exactly 7:00 p.m., Phillips comes to Jones and says, briefcase in hand as he's preparing to leave, "Chicago isn't agreeing to this number, but by God, if I can get them to commit to it, will you accept it?" And Jonesy says yes.

The settlement was 65 cents on the dollar: $14.7 million.

On the way out the door, one of the investors turns to Jones and asks, "Do you think we could have gotten 67?"

*** ***

CHAPTER 22

Most Investors Choose Litigation

Why settle for nickels when you think they owe you dollars?

Part 1: Litigation

Three large financial institutional investors participated in and lent money into the program: Ovation Finance, Banc of California, and CalPrivate. Each of them had filed a lawsuit against Chicago Title, and by and large, their litany of wrongs and grievances were uniform and consistent.

To give you just a small taste of the nature of the litigation, I'm going to share various claims from each of the lawsuits. Please remember that just because one lawyer says one thing doesn't necessarily make it so. Point made.

Ovation Finance is a large investment group out of Texas. In fairness to Ovation, these guys were not beginners. They had more than $500 million under management, and they are a sophisticated financial company.

When the fraud was exposed, they expressed some thoughts from their lawsuit (the comments in parentheses are mine):

40. "Ovation Finance's business strategy principally entails private market lending. In mid-2017, Kim Funding (Kim Peterson) presented the ANI Loan Program opportunity to Ovation. The ANI Loan Program seemed attractive to Ovation because it afforded a 10 percent rate of return without placing the principal at significant risk."

(Risk is a financial concept open to interpretation. Black Swans can arrive at any time.)

41. "As part of its diligence, Ovation requested confirmation that the funds for the applicants' escrow would, in fact, be held in escrow accounts in the name of Ovation Finance and controlled by Chicago Title. On June 27, 2017, Peterson provided a June 23, 2017, e-mail from Betty Elixman ('Elixman'), an escrow officer at Chicago Title, to Champion-Cain, representing that 'we were at 301 escrows totaling $61,370,000.' The e-mail was sent from betty.elixman@chicagotitle escrows.com."

(Gentlemen, did you really look at the signature line? It doesn't look like @CTT.com, so this might be considered a red flag.)

43. "Ovation also spoke on several occasions with attorneys representing Kim Funding. One of these attorneys—a leading specialist in California alcoholic beverage regulation—provided a letter opining on the legality of the escrow arrangement under California alcoholic beverage laws. Another lawyer explained that based on the way the ANI Loan Program was structured, the only credit risk to the lender's principal was if Chicago Title effectively committed fraud or somehow exposed the escrow accounts to third parties."

Let's imagine that we're sitting in the Ovation Finance boardroom, we're about to go all in for $25 million, and a junior analyst points to the above-stated risk. The other members of the investment committee look at him with a certain disdain. *Come on, what are the odds of fraud and mismanagement at Chicago Title?*

The junior analyst points out that the group needs to admit that the risk is at least greater than zero, and he's chastised for his concern. The committee is set to give the go signal, and again the junior analyst raises his hand and asks the members if they're aware of the Rollo Norton Case involving Chicago Title and its role in fraudulently obtaining loans for a condominium project: Norton, who pleaded guilty to mail fraud in 2008, testified that an escrow officer and a local office supervisor at Chicago Title knew that what they were doing was wrong. In June 2010, a California state court-ordered Fidelity National [Chicago Title's parent company] to pay $5.7 million in punitive damages.

In one of those "You can't make this stuff up" moments, the attorney for the plaintiffs in that case was none other than Michael Kirby, who, while standing outside the courtroom in front of the reporters, said, "We're pleased that the jury found clear and convincing evidence that Chicago Title employees participated in this fraud."

At this point in the board meeting, our junior analyst will be thanked for his research and then sent out to pick up some turkey sandwiches. After all, lightning never strikes in the same place twice. And, after all, it *is* a solid, risk-free 10 percent return.

But life has a way, doesn't it? And ten years later—you guessed it—the same Michael Kirby is representing more than 35 individual investors who are suing Chicago Title as part of the liquor-license Ponzi scheme.

Déjà vu all over again? This guy was already 1–0 against the spread. If you're Chicago, are you sure you really want to call a blitz?

And as for that junior analyst, he's probably now working at Goldman Sachs.

44. "On July 16, 2017, Ovation's investment committee approved the transaction, a loan agreement for a $25 million line of credit."

49. "Also, on July 17, 2017, Kim Funding made its first funding request to Ovation Finance, for an initial $10 million draw on the line of credit. Kim Funding's request attached fifty-two executed Form Escrows. Each listed an individual applicant, a license number, and was signed by Champion-Cain on behalf of ANI and by Elixman on behalf of Chicago Title. The agreements were delivered in two e-mails. The e-mail threads originated with Elixman's putative e-mail address at betty.elixman@chicagotitleescrows.com, and were forwarded, first through Champion Cain and then Peterson, to Ovation."

(There *is* that pesky email, courtesy of Kim and his desire to make an additional couple percent in interest payments. Stuff sure does come back to haunt, doesn't it?)

50. "On July 19, 2017, before Ovation Finance initiated its first wire transfer to Chicago Title, counsel for Ovation asked Peterson if there was someone at Chicago Title who could confirm that Ovation Finance's principal would be safeguarded in separate escrow accounts under which funds could not be released without its consent. Ovation, however, insisted that, because of the amount of money at issue, it would not fund prior to speaking live with someone from Chicago Title. Peterson eventually set up a conference call between Ovation, Champion-Cain, and DuCharme for the following day."

51. "On July 20, 2017, at noon central time, Ovation's Chief Financial Officer and its Vice President of Finance and Accounting initiated the conference call. First, they called Champion-Cain. Then Ovation added DuCharme to the call, having already confirmed that the telephone number provided for her was a listed number in Chicago Title's San Diego offices."

52. "After introductions, Ovation's CFO explained that Ovation was about to wire Chicago Title $10 million and he wanted to be sure that the money would be safely handled to ensure that Ovation was wiring to a Chicago Title escrow in Ovation's name that Ovation controlled. DuCharme confirmed that Chicago Title would be placing the money in an escrow account in Ovation's name. Ovation's CFO then confirmed the names of the entities sending and receiving the

wire, the account and wire information, and the escrow number that was printed on the top of each of the escrow agreements Ovation had received from Kim Funding three days prior; DuCharme confirmed these details. Following the call, Ovation believed that the safety of its deposit was ensured."

(Now, this is the moment when we're reminded of one of the great lawyers in American jurisprudence, Groucho Marx, who asked, "Who you going to believe, me or your lyin' eyes?"

The issue of individual escrow accounts was a consistent source of confusion and misunderstanding for the investors. DuCharme did confirm that Chicago Title would be placing the money in an escrow account in the lender's [Ovation's] name, but that's not exactly how it really worked. In practice, the funds wired from Ovation went into a Master Escrow Agreement, and ostensibly, within that account, there were little baskets labeled with your name, which license you'd invested in, and perhaps a reminder as to when your birthday was so that Chicago could send a card, but there were *never*, ever individual escrow accounts for each license.

During the entire seven years of the program, I think it's fair to say that many investors, if not most, were under the impression that they had their own individual cubby, sort of like a private locker at the golf club, when in fact, that was impossible because I was selling the same license number multiple times.

You go to get your clubs on Sunday, and, WTF, you find that someone else is using them.)

56. "Ultimately, between July 20, 2017, and August 8, 2019, Ovation Finance wired thirty-one tranches of loans to Chicago Title, purportedly to fund 255 liquor license application escrows arranged by ANI."

57. "On January 17, 2018, Ovation's auditors, KPMG, sent an audit confirmation letter to DuCharme at Chicago Title. They wanted confirmation that their $25 million was being 'held in escrow' per the attached list of 123 different escrows, by license number, funding date and amount, etc. DuCharme checked the box 'correct.'"

(But Ovation and KPMG weren't done. They also asked for a phone-call confirmation. Unbeknownst to Ovation, I'd arranged with DuCharme to preview that call and what to say, and literally, when Ovation called and DuCharme was on the phone with them, I was standing right behind her, making sure she said the right things. I pulled this right out of *Dial M for Murder*.)

64. "As of September 30, 2020, $23.4 million of Ovation Finance's principal that was supposed to be safely sitting in escrow accounts protected by Chicago Title, as well as $4.1million in interest, has not been returned."

(In fairness to Ovation, short of walking into the building followed by six large men wearing balaclavas and carrying assault rifles, and then standing in front of DuCharme's desk, it would be hard to argue that Ovation wasn't diligent in their review efforts.

As a "thank-you" after the fact, I sent $13,000 to Della DuCharme and $5,000 to Betty Elixman, who said, "You are the nicest, kindest, sweetest person I have ever met. Thank you so much for the gift, it brought tears to my eyes."

So does slicing onions.)

Part 2: Litigation

Kim Peterson had just brought Ovation Finance into the program for $25 million, but when you're printing money, you don't want to run out of ink. Next up for Peterson was Banc of California. He went to them looking for another $25–$30 million.

The Banc gave Peterson a commitment letter for a $25 million line of credit and a couple years later, they, too, along with Ovation Finance, found that their money had disappeared. They hired the same lawyers, Kirkland and Ellis, to share some of their own well-considered thoughts with Chicago Title. You have to admire their fiscal prudence, saving on legal fees.

From the Banc of California lawsuit (the comments in parentheses are mine):

65. "In mid-2017, Peterson and Kim Funding presented the ANI Loan Program opportunity to Banc of California. The ANI Loan Program seemed attractive to Banc of California because the funds were to be deposited directly into an escrow account at Chicago Title where Banc of California was to be named as a third-party beneficiary with an ownership interest in the deposited funds."

66. "In response to Banc of California's initial due diligence requests, on August 1, 2017, Peterson provided the June 23, 2017, e-mail from Elixman at the betty.elixman@chicagotitleescrows.com that had previously been provided to Ovation. As noted, the e-mail explained that 'we were at 301 escrows totaling $61,370,000.'"

(Of course, what was not noted or observed was that the domain @ chicagotitleescrows.com wasn't owned by Chicago Title, but rather was owned by me.)

67. "In addition, Banc of California hired an outside auditor to perform a books and records audit of ANI escrows and the records of Kim Funding. The auditor, Belinda Gisbert, confirmed to Banc of California that an e-mail from Chicago Title dated October 17, 2017, showed that the 'balance is $83,930,000 with 397 escrows.'"

(As you can see, business was booming.)

68. "On September 28, 2017, Banc of California sent Kim Funding a commitment letter offering a $25 million line of credit, whose purpose was to provide 'bridge financing for ABC loans.'"

70. "The Loan Documents provided capital for the financing of escrow deposits as required by California Alcoholic Beverage Control Act, in connection with the sale/transfer of liquor licenses."

(You will continue to note that the concept of single, unique escrows gets conflated with the Master Escrow Agreement, over which I had complete control.)

74. "On November 9, 2017, Kim Funding made its first funding request to Banc of California, for an initial $3.2 million draw on the line of credit. Kim Funding's request attached fourteen executed escrow agreements in the form specified in the Loan Agreement. Each listed an individual applicant, a license number, and was signed by Champion-Cain on behalf of ANI and by Elixman on behalf of Chicago Title."

(This claim is a bit nuanced. In order to facilitate sending out a couple thousand escrows and receipts for money wired to Chicago, I had some signature stamps made up, one for each of the key ladies, Betty and Della. So technically, Joelle in my office inked the documents, but she used the stamp that had their name on it. I never "signed" anything.)

77. "As certain of the loans were purportedly repaid, Kim Funding would provide new escrows into which Banc of California would then re-loan money."

(In Vegas, this is as known as "Press the 8" or "Let it ride" or "Baby needs a new pair of shoes." Let me remind you of the wise words of Bernard Baruch: "Nobody ever lost money taking a profit.")

78. "In April 2018, as part of its internal audit, Banc of California required one of its relationship managers, Lindy Mamer, to 'touch base' with DuCharme at Chicago Title:

> Hi Kim and Gina,
>
> *We have an internal audit and they have asked if I have spoken directly to Della as an 'extra' check that we are dealing with Chicago Title. Yes, I know we are because the process is working smoothly."*

(Are you kidding me? For this kind of money, do you think it would not go smoothly? I was buying WD-40 by the gallon, no friction.)

Mamer's email continues:

> "But just to answer the auditors, I would like to just touch bases with Della. Would that be okay? And if so, can you send me her email and phone number? Thank you, thank you!!
>
> Lindy Mamer
>
> Senior Vice President, Senior Relationship Manager
>
> Commercial Banking"

(The Banc is sending in millions of dollars, and Lindy has to use exclamation points to show appreciation? After all, whose money is it?)

> Five minutes later, I reply by email:
>
> *"Sure!! Do you want email or phone? She has two email addresses they use for internal and external lines of business or maybe you want to just call her? Let me know so I can give her heads up you are calling to just introduce yourself and to satisfy your auditors that she actually exists. Ha-ha ☺"*

(Of course every policeman calls in advance to make an appointment to let you know when he'll be knocking on your door, looking for the cocaine and the loaded gun. But Lindy Mamer is smart. She's not going down easily.)

> "I think both. I should talk to her to verify her voice (if I ever have to call her in the future) and an email so I can have it in writing for the file."

(Lindy, if you've never talked to her, how are you going to verify her voice? This is the stuff of Perry Mason, 60 years ago. I tell Lindy that Della is very busy—she's in and out a lot.)

> *"But she will be available at her office phone anytime between 9:30 am and 11 am* **tomorrow**. *Do you want to give me a time when you want to buzz her, so I can let her know to*

*make sure she doesn't step out of the office unexpectedly? She
is really a busy lady."*

(Elmore Leonard stuff. Please advise the bank teller when you'll be
arriving to rob the joint so she can have the small, unmarked bills
nicely packaged, and turn off the alarm. Lindy confirms 9:30 a.m. for
the call. And then I send her an email response.)

> "By the way I did confirm with her that this is just a quick
> intro call so you can introduce yourself. As you recall
> from your dealings with Kim, if you have any questions
> regarding the program, you need to go directly through
> me. There is a strict protocol for this program due to the
> fact that we have many different lenders and thus, Chicago
> Title's Master Escrow Holding Agreement is with ANI
> Development, LLC.
>
> "There are confidentiality and fiduciary issues at stake,
> and Chicago Title seemingly acting for multiple parties
> can face difficult challenges even when these parties are
> of a single, non-conflicting class."

(In any normal world, this would look liked an IED with a ribbon
on it. But I'd gone to law school, so I knew how to sling some scary
words. I admit I was pushing the envelope. Too much nosing around,
Ms. Mamer, and your bank will be out in the cold.)

My email continued:

> "If you have specific requests, always put these in writing to
> me, and I, in turn, will forward to Betty/Della at Chicago
> Title for them to answer. I need everything in a paper trail
> for this program as you can imagine."

(I think I was channeling the Nigerian Prince program. And then I
went Full Monty.)

"All the other lenders (including banks like yours) follow this protocol. Again, we are very lucky Della works with us on this deal. I never want that to change. Thanks Lindy,"

Lindy was dutiful, made the call to Della, and reported to the Banc that "the escrow process was going well."

But Kim wasn't satisfied with the first deal; he wanted to go back for more. I had a lot of thoughts on the question of when is enough, enough, and I'll probably have a few years in prison to contemplate that.

In the summer of 2018, Kim wanted to borrow some more money on his line at Banc of California, expanding it up to the maximum of $35 million. In response, Banc of California figured it needed some expanded due diligence, so it brought in one of its big guns, Steve Cusato, Senior Vice President, Market Executive, Commercial Banking.

Cusato wrote to Kim:

"I have assembled a team within the Banc to expand our due diligence of Chicago Title. Of course, their financial statements and that of their parent are available publicly and I have made sure they have been available internally.

"I think where we are going is more towards a kick the tires and understand their internal control procedures. I think if we understood their process flow (high level) from start to finish that would work Specifically the controls that are in place for the movement of money back and forth between you and Chicago. In addition, the segregation between your escrow and the sister escrow."

(Cusato must have been thinking of the music group Sister Sledge. As I touched on earlier, there was no such thing as a sister escrow. I'd made up this whole idea early on to explain to Kim why some licenses in Northern California didn't have the right numbers, and certain Form 226s hadn't been filed by Chicago. *Sister escrow* is the same as *snipe hunt*.)

Cusato went on:

> "The team in addition to myself will be a senior credit
> officer that specifically works with financial institutions,
> internal legal and a senior operations officer.
>
> "My feeling is that it would not take but a couple of hours.
> I would like the final internal report to say: 'Chicago is very
> professional with good controls and safeguards, experienced
> professionals, and all levels; they have the balance sheet
> to back up their operations and a parent company that
> provides additional back up. We are comfortable that the
> collateral funds we have at their institution are safe and
> sound and we consider the risk minimal and acceptable
> for the commitment we are considering.'"

(Cusato, there *is* such a thing as an open-book test, but why do that
when you can go all in and just give them the answers to the test?
That way you don't have to waste time grading it.)

The lawsuit continued:

88. "On September 19, 2018, relationship managers Mamer and Steve
Cusato ('Cusato') visited DuCharme and Elixman at Chicago Title's
office and met DuCharme and Elixman in person. Mamer stated later,
'We discussed the reporting and their compliance by the State which
sounds almost as extensive as our bank regulations.'"

Cusato sent an email to Della:

> "Thank you for all your hard work. Sorry we did not get
> to say 'hi' when we stopped by earlier with the flowers
> and cookies. We hope you enjoy them. Lindy and I real-
> ize that we have been a bit needy with our report request
> and wanted to say thank you. Our external auditors are
> driving us all crazy. Your verification should put them at
> bay (same one you do for CalPrivate)."

(Cusato was unfailingly polite. After all, since you're going to fleece us for about $30 million, it seems only common decency for us to apologize for wanting to know how you're going to do it. And then he delivered the coup de grace, the one that will live in infamy.)

> "I know I speak for the whole Banc in saying your professionalism is impressive and exemplary and a critical component for our involvement in the overall relationship.

> Thank you again for helping us and all you do.

> — *Steve Cusato, SVP Market Executive*
> *Commercial Banking"*

(And my girls were equally polite and charming.)

Della responded by email:

> *"I apologize, I was on a lengthy conference call, please let me know when you are going to stop by, I am happy to make some time. We really appreciate the beautiful flowers and delicious cookies can never have too many of those. Many thanks, have a great day! Della DuCharme."*

(It's at this point that one might consider taking all of one's money out of Banc of California.)

More from the lawsuit:

92. "As of September 30, 2020, Banc of California lost $35.525 million in principal that should have been safely sitting in escrow accounts protected by Chicago Title."

93. "Unfortunately for ANI's lenders, the entire ANI Loan Program was a fraudulent scheme."

94. "There were no liquor license applicants applying for loans from ANI."

(That is the moment of truth when the Fat Lady ascends to the stage, removes her cape, spritzes her throat, and lets forth with an "A" above high "C."

Lots of people went to the bedroom and looked under the covers, but they weren't very good at it. They needed to look under the sheets, because when you want to believe what you want to believe, well, you end up just becoming a true believer.)

Part 3: Litigation

From the litigation: *CALPRIVATE BANK v. CHICAGO TITLE:*

1. "Beginning in September 2015 and continuing through June 2019, CalPrivate Bank advanced over 40 million dollars to a San Diego-based company, ANI License Fund, LLC controlled by San Diego socialite Gina Champion-Cain."

(Personally, I take offense at the word *socialite*. I've always been a working girl, not a lady who lunches.

CalPrivate Bank's story is the same old story—a fight for love and glory. The bank was originally called San Diego Private Bank, and it was where Kim Peterson went for his first tranche of institutional money. He initially borrowed $5 million on a Business Loan Agreement line of credit. Later, he increased the line to $12.5 million.

CalPrivate recounts asking Peterson, "After receiving the first set of escrow agreements to be funded, why did the names on the list of liquor licenses being transferred not match the Individual Liquor License Escrow Agreements?"

And then while awaiting the answer from Peterson, they asked the same question of Chicago Title. The question got routed from Della to me. I responded.)

37. "Hi, Sasha [the bank loan administrator], escrow called to tell me you asked for the information directly from them. I really need you to go directly through me on these matters and not reach out to Escrow as I handle the lawyers and Escrow deals through me."

38. "Ultimately, Plaintiff (CalPrivate Bank) was redirected to Peterson for an explanation, who falsely told Plaintiff that the names on the list of applicants did not match those on the Individual Liquor License Escrow Agreements because the former is the name of the existing license owner and not the applicant."

(At this point, several red flags should have fallen from the bank's ceiling, but the cleaning crew must have picked them up before anyone noticed, and the bank went all in.

As I read these lawsuits, I'm still amazed that the program lasted for seven years. Inspector Clouseau could have figured it out. I wanted the merry-go-round to stop, but no one seemed to know where the off switch was.

Fees, irrational returns, greed, stupidity, fees, money—that's what makes the merry-go-round . . . go round.)

The last line of the lawsuit:

63. "None of the $12,475,000 in loan advances have been repaid to Plaintiff."

"This is Ripley, last survivor of the *Nostromo*, signing off."

*** ***

CHAPTER 23

A Software Genius

"Software is eating the world."
—venture capitalist Marc Andreessen

I t was going to take some sophisticated software to keep track of all the money, the in and the out, the term and the rate, and so on. When people (and the lawyers) looked back on the run, they were the most impressed by the tracking system I'd developed. The whole system was compartmentalized by investor, by bundler, by commission, by rollover term, by who knew whom and the need to keep the story consistent. I was very detailed. My spreadsheets were impeccable, and the reason no one ever complained was because everyone got paid "like clockwork."

But on the other side of the ledger, the bundler side, some of those guys weren't doing as well in terms of details, and keeping track of the money was becoming a challenge.

Synapse Development, one of the companies that raised money for me, was drowning in their yellow-pad-paper scoring system, so they set out to hire a young software developer to work on a program for tracking all the licenses and the loans they had on the books. I became friendly with him, and here's a bit of his story. Let's call him "Peter."

Peter: "The fund hired me to build a software program to manage the loans they were issuing. They only had the most rudimentary spreadsheet, and they needed a better way to keep track of all the money and produce proper financial statements for the investors.

"They were classic clients with unreasonable expectations. The engagement was initially only going to be the standard what can you do for me in three months. But then they liked what they saw and wanted to add more bells and whistles. I ended up working on the software for them for almost four years, until the whole thing fell apart."

That was kid's stuff for this guy; in my mind, I saw even more greatness in Peter. He mostly dealt with Joelle Hanson and Cris Torres, who both worked for me at ANI, and they were the ones responsible for calculating and creating the IRS 1099s that were sent to each fund manager or individual lender to record the interest income received. This was time-consuming and complicated, so I decided to reach out to Peter, asking him to build a program to streamline this step of the program for us.

An IRS 1099 is the record of a payment (in this case, it was primarily interest income) that someone receives on an investment, and a copy is sent to the IRS so that they know what you were paid, and subsequently, the amount of tax that may be due.

Nota bene: The IRS document that is sent to you for your tax reporting is identical to the one being sent to the IRS; they have to match.

My company was responsible for sending out all the 1099s for all the investors Here's why there was some complexity to the process:

The Synapse managers wanted to track *all* of the licenses in a given tranche—let's call the number 19 in total—even though their fund may have only picked eight for their clients.

I told Peter that we would be responsible to send out the 1099s to his eight investors and to file them with the IRS with a record of what interest they received. But instead, Peter would send me the interest-income numbers for all 19 investors in the tranche, assuming that everyone was created equal. This created a problem because every investor/bundler had a slightly different deal. When the 19 arrived, I had to separate Peter's group of 8 from the other group of 11, and then shred those 11 and create new 1099s for those 11 investors with the proper interest number. In the end, all 19 were filed correctly. And never the twain shall meet.

Peter was a true entrepreneur, and he reasoned that maybe this same IRS 1099 software program might be really valuable to Chicago Title. They were a very manual shop without very sophisticated processes, and he had this idea to create a spin-out to license the software to Chicago as a SaaS (software as a service) platform, to automate the entire process.

I told him that it was a brilliant idea, but I didn't think Chicago would give up on their archaic ways. They were stuck in the mud from 20 years ago in terms of programming. I told him that when we wanted them to run off a balance sheet or a statement for us showing how many people had wired in and how much money was in each account, they had to do it manually, going through each receipt one at a time.

If I were to show this to Chicago, it would be like putting a neutron bomb on my program—only a matter of time until boom—and goodbye. And although I admired Peter's entrepreneurial spirit, this idea needed to be shut down. Which I did.

After my plea deal in September, I had a chance to catch up with Peter for a coffee. He'd moved on to another company writing code for them.

Peter: "You know, I was never sure about your numbers. I did point out to the promoters when I started working for them that the data we were getting was always from you, signed by Della or Betty. There was no perfect way for me to cross-compare against the escrows at Chicago. And frankly, the management team at the fund seemed less concerned with mathematical accuracy and more interested in their billing fees. I hate to say it, but they never really did the math to figure out how there could ever be enough money for everyone."

Me: "Their fees over the course of the deal were $2.6 million."

Peter: "And the sad part was that I didn't believe my own numbers. I'm always nervous if I can't figure out how a deal really works. If the promoters had carefully considered who got paid from whom and for how much, they would have quickly seen that mathematically you would be losing money on every transaction, if you were paying their fees from your share of the 'profit.' It didn't add up.

"And to add insult to injury, I invested $1.8 million of my own money in your program, and to date, I've gotten nothing back. Of course, I did receive interest payments, but I rolled those all back in. You know, I saw the data, and everything looked real. But what really surprised me was how many other groups had put in money that we had no idea about. We were only a small fraction."

Me: "I didn't know you invested. I'm sorry."

Peter: "Well, I'm in one of the lawsuits against you and Chicago Title, so we'll see."

*** ***

CHAPTER 24

Till Death Do Us Part

Don't marry the one you can live with; marry
the one you can't live without.

If you Google the word *marriage*, you get 1.85 *billion* results, so
clearly this is a topic that seems to interest people. And if you
Google the word *divorce*, you get 3.1 *billion* results. I guess people
keep doing it over and over until they get it right.

I've now been married to Steve Cain for 30 years. What can I tell
you—some things were just meant to be. He's tall and handsome and
charming and has a sardonic sense of humor. We used to laugh a lot.
I got lucky. But marriage is more complicated than a Ponzi scheme.
He had his business in Mexico, and I had mine in San Diego. And I
was good at compartmentalizing. I'd instructed my employees that if
Steve ever came into the office, they were to dummy up, close up the
books, and discuss nothing other than the weather. I *never* wanted
him to get involved.

People have asked me, "Did he know?" The answer is *no*, not ever.
That is, not until August 28, 2019, after I came home from the plea-
agreement meeting with the SEC in Los Angeles.

That was an interesting night, I assure you. It was painful. Steve asked me what I'd been thinking for the last seven years, and I had no answer. But he confessed to me that he'd fallen in love with me for exactly some of the qualities that had brought me down. He loved my optimism and my energy, and the fact that I was always going forward, with no impediments. Relentless, determined, charismatic. But there was darkness. He asked me again why I'd put my life and his life at risk. It wasn't like we were poor and living in a homeless shelter.

Long before I'd ever seen a liquor license, we'd built a life, we'd bought a house, and we had a full life together. And he could now see that house beginning to crumble in front of his eyes. On that night, I thought back to The Patio on Lamont. The hard questions are easy to answer now: *Would one good restaurant have been enough? Why did I need an empire?*

We all know about women who marry felons in prison, and we know about prisoners who get divorced, either because of the wife's desire to do so or as a choice to free the other. I know that Steve feels betrayed, but I'm not getting a life sentence, so I'll have to leave the final decision to Steve on that one. I think we'll stay married, but who knows?

But allow me a moment to be a tiny bit unfair. After all, for 28 of those 30 years, we had a hell of a ride. It wasn't all bad. Steve is a Boy Scout, and if he'd understood the whole story early in the game, he would have shut it down in a heartbeat. We lived large, but the truth is that it was more for me than it was for him. I think, at times, that he kept me company just because he loved me. He had a relatively famous wife—toast-of-the-town stuff—but it never mattered to him. The La Jolla Beach and Tennis Club and all the fancy political fundraisers and charity events were not his scene.

I have a friend who's very wealthy, charming, and kind. His wife is forbidden from ever entering the building he owns. They've been married for 32 years and have three wonderful children. You think you know, but "you don't know jack."

As I prepare for prison, my focus is pretty mundane: find a place for the dogs, get all the documents and passwords Steve will need in one place, and then clean out the storage bins and give away all the clothes—I *did* have a lot of clothes. I was still taking Big Tony to the Veterans Administration hospital for his medications, and I got some dental work done since I'm told dental care in prison is pretty sketchy. I don't like leaving loose ends. And, of course, I do cook dinner for Steve every night. It sounds like every other old married couple, except for the prison thing.

I look back on the last seven years, and I'm puzzled. I can't really understand it. It just wasn't me. My sister sent me an email with an incredible line in it: "What breaks my heart the most is that you thought so little of your life that you would do this to yourself."

My sister will never understand. I don't think poorly of myself. I love my life. I'm a very happy, optimistic person. But I still don't understand what in God's name compelled me to step out of my norm to such an extreme. Such a wildly crazy extreme. I just don't know.

*** ***

CHAPTER 25

Reflections
and Remorse

The cruelest word in the English language: *If*

There's no refuge from memory in this world. Your brain is a crumpled sheet of some 86 billion neurons—no wonder we do stupid things.

It's beyond the comprehension of almost everyone who ever knew me that I could have done this. I've been asked multiple times why, how, when, and then why again. What motivated me to commit this crime?

I was seen by many as a "woman who had it all." I was an example of making it in a "man's world." But perception and reality often diverge; it only appeared that way. It took maximum effort on my part to continue to appear to have it all when I really *didn't* have it all, and to continue to present a front to the world that wasn't real.

Each of us balances our view of ourselves against what we think the world's view of us is. Keeping up appearances is daunting. Consider the real estate agent who leases a $90,000 BMW that she can't afford but has to have because you can't show a client a $3 million home if you pick them up at the airport in a 2014 Dodge minivan.

Like many people, I was struggling during and after the 2009 financial debacle. If you're a developer and there are no deals and there's no financing, well, you have choices, and none of them are thrilling to you.

The same is true of just about all professionals. For example, lawyers who need to appear bigger than they are because they're fishing for blue fin, and you can't go fishing for that-size fish if your office is in the back of a nail salon (see *Better Call Saul*). You need custom shirts with your initials on the cuffs.

I knew this syndrome up close and personal. In the early '90s, I was considered a "player" in the downtown San Diego real estate market. I knew the drill. You get something under contract, then go outside, throw up, and then start dialing for dollars to close. It was always a race to the finish line—only just a few steps ahead of the grim reaper.

You don't see the best deals unless it's perceived that you can actually perform. So it's the tap dance of perception versus reality, and appearances matter. And if you're found to be a fraud or you disappoint the guys who bring you the deals more than a couple of times, then you're a dead woman walking and the thing you do—deals—well, you don't get to do them anymore. It's who you are. And it was who *I* was and wanted to remain.

But as the next chapter of my life begins, I truly understand how tenuous one's grasp of reality can be.

There were countless times when I wanted this program to stop. As soon as it began, I wanted it to stop. When I did that initial list of fake licenses for around $600,000, I thought that I could get out of it easily: *I'll refinance Lamont, and I just need this little bridge to get me through the next six months.*

But the dark truth is that while The Patio was viewed as a smashing success, it still lost money every month for a long time. Over the seven years after the first Patio, I opened another dozen restaurants, and none of them really made any money. The restaurant business is brutal, and

I wasn't that good at running them. I was brilliant at promoting and singing a song of possibilities and serving fabulous food, but ask the guy who ran point-of-sale technology for me. He'll tell you that the restaurants all lost money. We had to feed them every month, and I took the feed from the Master Escrow Account at Chicago Title.

I simply couldn't get food and labor and all that stuff under control. That was never my strong suit, and there was never anyone else who could do it. As long as I could feed the beast, I could hope that deliverance would arrive at some later date before the food spoiled. This illusion of success fueled my ability to seek more success, and I needed to believe that I could outrun the inevitable. The house of cards was going to need a new dealer eventually.

I told myself that I'd never take in more than $4 million. That amount I could pay back, but then, just like the drug addict who promises that this is his last hit, I couldn't stop. The license money poured into Chicago Title like a tsunami. I didn't even know the names of most of the investors—people I'd never heard of or met simply wired money.

It was a raging river, I was in a raft, and frankly, I wasn't sure where the waterfall was. But on the way down, it was a hell of an intoxicating ride. People were happy, they were all making lots of money, I was employing people, serving on civic boards, making charitable contributions. I was famous. Until I was infamous.

Each of us has a story that propels us forward. I was always taken by the story of football star Tom Brady. We both went to Michigan. He was picked in the sixth round of the 2000 NFL draft, making him 199th out of a total of 254 choices.

Much has been written about his anger and his need to show everyone that they were wrong. He's quite open about his feelings, and in a video, *Brady 6*, he's able to name every other quarterback picked ahead of him. Holding back just the hint of tears, he says that he's carried that humiliation of being picked so late, and it's what has motivated and fueled his desire to achieve, and has led to his ultimate greatness.

Brady was disrespected. And in my own way, I've carried that anger of being a woman—marginalized, excluded, and being underestimated. I used the liquor-license-program money to fund the business empire that I'd always wanted, which I thought I couldn't achieve otherwise. In my story, it was shoplifting on a grand scale.

I remember a man I worked with at the Resolution Trust Corporation in the 1990s. One day he took me aside and told me that women can be assertive in business, but they can't be aggressive, which frankly made no sense to me. But one thing I remember him telling me was: "Unfortunately for you, Gina, because you're a woman and because you're an *attractive* woman, you'll need to be the smartest person in the room at all times, and that's the only way you're gonna be successful in this male-dominated world." This man was a raving chauvinist, but he was telling me the truth.

He knew the guys that I worked with in that office weren't as clever as I was, but they all made more money, and they had different perks than I did. However, I worked twice as hard as they did, and he knew that. And I think that set me up for something that was very important throughout the rest of my career: I always worked harder than anybody else. And I enjoyed it. Working to me was always a giant puzzle to decipher, and I enjoyed being industrious and solving problems.

What ultimately drove me to start my own real estate business was the continued downward pressure I felt at the Koll Company. No excuses, you understand, but the white male culture just didn't bring out the best in me. I figured I was better suited to take my show on the road.

Whether it's revenge or redemption that we seek, each of us chases our own dream. It was what I did, and the reason they're called dreams and not reality is that they don't exist yet in real time. They're the fantasies and ghosts and chimeras of our desires. We attempt to create them and make them real, to breathe life into them; and in so doing, we pile up these small bricks, one by one, which in the end represent the structure that we call our own lives.

But when we come up a bit short on the dream and the creation, when the pass is intercepted, when reality comes knocking on the door, or more accurately, comes and knocks the door completely off its hinges, how we handle that loss or that rejection is the defining moment. And this moment is often hard to see, because giving up a dream isn't pleasant. It calls into question all the decisions in the past as well as the hopes for the future that didn't materialize.

Entrepreneurs will tell you and themselves that they're not doing it again for the money, but that's only partially the truth. Money helps you keep score, but what we really want is the power and the fame. It's being known and respected and held in high regard. And if the cards fall wrong, then the only way to prop up that dream is to take even *more* chances, fueled by desperation. And as the losses pile up, there's no way out.

I was haunted by the impostor syndrome. I'm not the first person to pick the illegal shortcut, and I sure won't be the last.

*** ***

CHAPTER 26
My CFO
Gets Sentenced

Collateral damage.

I recently watched a Netflix series called *Heist*. It's the story of a team of criminals who pull off a Brink's-like truck robbery in Spain, and what I liked was that one of the male characters, in an effort to escape being found out, dressed up as an old woman in a wheelchair with a blonde wig.

That thought did cross my mind.

I wanted to attend the sentencing of my CFO, Cris Torres, and I considered going to the courtroom in disguise, but after a moment of madness, I concluded that this was an insane idea, so I sent a friend to give me a report. I wanted a small preview of how Judge Burns was going to handle my case.

I've watched more than my fair share of courtroom scenes on TV and in the movies. Some of them are hilarious, like in the film *My Cousin Vinny*, and some are dead serious, like in *The Trial of the Chicago 7*. But my friend had never been in a real criminal courtroom until she went to the sentencing that day. She went early to make sure she got in.

Most of the morning involved Judge Larry Burns putting people in prison for smuggling drugs across the border. They were men and women who'd made bad choices—if they even *had* a chance to make a choice.

For the most part, all the stories were similar. The individuals were approached in Mexico, offered some money, usually $2,000 to $3,000 to take drugs across the border in their cars, were told they wouldn't get caught because they were U.S. citizens, and the bundler/operative who convinced these people to put their lives at risk for some money essentially gave them a taco and sent them on their way—ultimately to jail in America.

My friend told me that the first case involved a young man who thought he was just delivering a car, but the trunk was filled with crack. Another was a woman with an autistic child, and she said she needed money for her kid's care. It wasn't the headline stuff of a cartel drug bust. It was the detritus of daily life if you were trapped with no money or owed money or you'd just given up on life and hoped that you might catch one break, enough to get a little breathing room. It was heartbreaking to hear the stories of what drove people to take this kind of risk. Three years against $3,000.

None of them pleaded not guilty. They were there for their sentencing, and Burns, who'd been a judge since 2003, went through the standard motions, reminding each of them, like a stern father, that they'd made a terrible mistake and that he had no choice but to follow sentencing guidelines and essentially break their hearts.

Just like you see in the movies, the defendant and his or her lawyer sat on one side, and on the other side were representatives of the U.S. Attorney's Office (USAO). The public defender explained the circumstances and begged for mercy or house arrest or a reduced sentence, anything that would mitigate their client's potential prison time. It was hard to watch the system at work. Yes, each of them had committed a crime; and no, none of them were masterminds or shot-callers, but all of them had gotten caught in a revolving door of sadness and loss and ignorance.

Burns moved along, spending about 35 to 40 minutes on each case. They tell you about getting your day in court, but let me tell you, you do not get a *day*—you get less than an hour . . . and then you get remanded.

After hearing each case, Burns gave his speech, checked the guidelines, and told the defendant the number of months to be served. He gave each of them a similar speech. He said that if there was no punishment, if there were no consequences, then people would ignore the law, and the government would be a toothless tiger. Burns made it sound like he had no choice, but even if that were true, even if the law was unyielding in the sentencing guidelines, they were still only guidelines, and it was for sure that Burns didn't show much leniency with these people.

During this process, a door on the side of the courtroom opened, and two U.S. Marshals came out. They stood straight against the wall waiting, and when the judge said that the ball game was over and now the defendant was remanded, the Marshals came in, and politely, even gently, helped the person stand up, then slapped on the handcuffs and led him or her away. No waving to friends or relatives, no last kiss goodbye—just the short perp walk, and a closing door.

It was well rehearsed, and given the many dozens, if not hundreds, of similar felony drug charges that were being prosecuted, it was nothing more than ordering a Reuben sandwich at The Cheese Shop.

Judge Burns was unrelenting on those first three cases, so it was an easy-money bet that when Cris's case came up, it wasn't going to go well for him.

My friend who was witnessing all this was a novice when it came to crime and punishment, and she'd never considered sentencing and doing penance and seeking redemption. She was a bit terrified sitting in the back of the courtroom. She told me that she never wanted to have to sit in judgment of another person. Holding someone's future life in your hands—that is a monumental responsibility.

She told me that when the young mother with the autistic child was sentenced to 37 months, it felt more like the judge was sentencing the *child* to prison, not the mother. Who was going to take care of the kid while her mom was in prison? Yes, I know that the mother might have thought about that prior to crossing with the drugs, but that's asking a lot of someone who's desperate and thinks she only has one option.

After dispensing justice upon the drug offenders, it was 11:30 a.m., and time to deal with Crispin Torres, who'd worked for me at ANI for more than 15 years and had been promoted to CFO (chief financial officer) in late 2015.

My friend took detailed notes, and later I read the transcript. The order of events is like this: There's a sentencing brief prepared by the USAO that takes into account the report of the probation officer. In essence, the probation report said that Torres was a minor player, knew he did wrong, had major health issues, and so on:

> "Mr. Torres knows that he must be punished for what he did in this case. It is the astronomical amount of money that Ms. Champion-Cain was able to steal from the investors in the lending program that drives the Sentencing Guidelines in this case and exposes Mr. Torres to a significant prison term. But the person who orchestrated the scheme and personally benefitted from it should bear the brunt of those Guidelines, not Mr. Torres. He has taken responsibility for his actions and he did so quickly and he has been as helpful in the criminal and civil cases as he could be. He will be liable for huge amounts of restitution that he will likely never be able to pay off in his lifetime. His career is over and his health is in decline. He is a convicted felon. Prison is not required in this case."

Next up is Ms. Ferrara, the attorney for Mr. Torres:

"But as time went on, Mr. Torres started to suspect that there weren't really any licenses, that the program was not real. He didn't see any paperwork about it and he couldn't understand how the program generated profits. And while he was friendly with Ms. Champion-Cain and loyal to her for his job, he was also afraid of her. He worried that she would fire him if he started digging into this lending program. He was weak and he knew that she knew he was weak and that he was dependent on her continued good will. So, he didn't question her.

"When he became very ill in 2015, first with tuberculosis and then later, in 2016, when he was diagnosed with Parkinson's disease, there was no discussion of him losing his job or being demoted.

"By 2016–2017, Mr. Torres knew that the businesses owned by ANI were failing. There was not enough money to pay the bills of the legitimate businesses—the restaurants and retail operations, especially. They had monthly shortfalls that they could not get loans to cover. So, Mr. Torres would email Ms. Champion-Cain and tell her that ANI needed money for expenses. And Ms. Champion-Cain would take money from the escrow account where the money from the investors to the lending program was deposited and direct him to use it to pay the expenses of ANI. Mr. Torres knew it was misappropriating funds but he felt powerless to do anything about it. He had to keep his job and his health insurance."

(As an important note, please understand firsthand how the power and fear of losing health insurance in America informs every part of one's life.)

More from Ms. Ferrara:

"Mr. Torres has been with his husband Dean for over 12 years, married for almost seven. He has Parkinson's and tuberculosis. He knows he committed a crime. He has pled guilty. This is why the Probation Office recommended that Torres not go to prison. This Court has the ability to sentence Mr. Torres to up to five years of probation or up to five years in prison, followed by up to three years of Supervised Release. For the reasons stated above, Mr. Torres asks the Court to sentence him to five years of probation, with one to two years of home confinement."

Now let's look at the sentencing memorandum from the U.S. Attorneys:

Drew Galvin, Assistant U.S. Attorney:

"Champion-Cain used at least $60 million of investor funds to prop up her other businesses, including restaurants, clothing stores, vacation rentals. Id., ¶ 11. Many of these businesses were failing, and some had negative cash flows. When the businesses were unable to meet their expenses, Defendant would ask Champion-Cain to wire money from the Escrow Company to American National Investments so that he could cover any shortfalls. Defendant knew that the money came from investors and that this was not a permissible use of their funds.

"As CFO, Defendant prepared Form 1099 statements for investors and vendors, worked with the company's outside accountants, applied for Small Business Administration loans, and supervised staff accountants. What it comes down to, Your Honor, is he was not—we have no evidence that he was aware of the fraudulent scheme. His role was limited to moving money from an escrow account into American National Investment's bank accounts.

"The Government has recommended six months in custody with one year of home confinement. See Government's Sentencing Memorandum, CM/ECF # 27.

"The United States recommends that the Court sentence Defendant to six months in prison and a three-year term of supervised release with a condition requiring twelve months of home detention."

Ms. Ferrara is allowed to speak:

"Thank you, Your Honor. I think it might help if I could inquire of the Court if—if the Court is inclined to follow the recommendation."

This is the moment where the two putts are each within six feet, and the golfers look at each other and propose to go with "Good . . . good," and "Let's move on to the next hole." In other words, Ms. Ferrara has essentially said, "Look, Judge, me and the U.S. Attorney, Mr. Galvin over there, we've made a deal, we've considered all the issues. I mean, come on, the guy is damn near the walking dead. He's physically frail, and this guy isn't going to last too long in the GPOP (general prison population), so to save the state some money and give this guy a break, we'll take the six months and call it a day. Will that work for you, Your Honor?"

My friend thought this was going to work out for Cris.

And then the judge spoke from on high, saying essentially: "No, it will not. That deal doesn't work for me. I have this giant Ponzi scheme case on my docket, and I'm going to make some examples, starting with your guy. If he were the CFO, he must have known, he should have known, and as far as I'm concerned, he knew."

My friend was squirming in her seat. Huh? The two sides made a deal, and you, in your wisdom, are going to ignore it and make a new deal?

So when I read the trial transcript, I tried to imagine what Cris might have said to the judge if he were allowed to speak at that time:

Hey, I pled guilty, we made a deal. That's why I admitted my guilt or complicity or whatever. You guys told me I would get an easy sentence if I cooperated. I cooperated; I told you everything I knew. I'm sick as a dog, I'm not a real CFO, I'm not even a CPA. Gimme a break. I wrote checks, okay, maybe I considered the word Ponzi, *but I didn't know for sure—she kept everything pretty tightly closed up. All I did was send checks where she told me to, and I know I did the wrong thing, I admit my guilt, but I needed the health insurance, and telling Gina that she was breaking the law was going to get me fired, so I hunkered down, did my job, and looked the other way. I know that was wrong, but Parkinson's is a bitch, and I have tuberculosis as well, and at the end of the day, I was nothing more than a bookkeeper; I was not a kingpin.*

When her regular businesses needed money for payroll, I told her, and she put some money in the account, and I paid the bills. I didn't ask too many questions. And then I made a deal with the U.S. government, that guy sitting over there, and now you're telling me you don't like the deal. If I can't trust my government, who can I trust?

At least that's what I would have said—or words to that effect.

And then Burns did some calculations, disregarded the recommendations, and mandated a sentence of 37 months in prison. Time for a lunch break.

My friend who knew Torres began to cry just a little bit. She was astounded by how the justice system seemed to work.

In the courtroom discussion, the judge repeatedly referred to me as the "kingpin," and to Torres as my willing henchman. I think maybe Burns had watched the movie *Scarface* too many times.

When Torres walked out of the courtroom, he fell into the arms of his husband, and they both began to cry softly at first and then sob loudly, holding each other for a very long time. My friend couldn't watch and had to turn and run down the hall to the elevators. She'd seen enough, and when she gave me her report, I knew that my ball game was in the bottom of the ninth.

*** ***

CHAPTER 27

My Sentencing

Everyone gets their day in court, but it usually
only lasts about an hour.

March 31, 2021

S o how did I spend my last night of freedom?

The night before my sentencing, I ran over to Siesel's Meats, our go-to butcher shop, and grabbed my favorite cut of meat, which is a ribeye. Stevo grilled it out on our beautiful deck high above Old Town, overlooking San Diego Bay, Mission Bay, and Mission Beach. The weather was perfect. I made a huge salad, a little wild rice, and we opened several bottles of fine red wine. I'd started my happy hour with a few girlfriends who came over earlier in the afternoon for champagne and cheese. The dogs, Stevo, and I enjoyed a beautiful evening together—at peace, relaxing, watching *Bosch* on Netflix. I slept like a baby that night.

Earlier that day, I'd walked the dogs, as I do every day. First, I took them to a grassy field in Mission Beach at Marina Village. It wasn't a dog park, per se, but I treated it as such, as I let our three dogs off leash there, and they chased balls, rolled around in the grass, and ran around like crazy while I got to look at the sailboats docked there.

On the way home, I did the turnaround at the World Famous restaurant in Mission Beach, watched the waves, and then headed back home with the dogs.

I'd arranged for all three dogs, Rocky (nine), Enzo (seven), and Sophia (three), to be adopted by three wonderful families. I'd planned ahead, figuring that Judge Burns was going to remand me that same morning.

My lawyers picked me up at 8:30 a.m. I selected a classy yet comfortable black dress and sweater in case I was immediately remanded—one I didn't care if they "destroyed," yet one that was timeless and professional. I wore no jewelry, as I'd been instructed as such. Although Steve wanted to come to the courthouse, I told him no, that he could not. What was the purpose of him seeing me being put in handcuffs and led out through that door?

I gave Steve a kiss and got in the car, and off I went with my lawyers. I'm not a big one for long goodbyes, and I told myself that this was an important next step in my life journey. I was ready for it—almost excited—but I knew that I'd be back. I wasn't planning on dying in prison. I've come to learn during my time incarcerated that most folks have the same reaction: "Let's get on with it."

As I walked into the courtroom, I was thinking of my family and friends, worrying about them, as I knew that Judge Burns would give me the max sentence. I'd been warned about that over and over again by friends of mine who were local criminal lawyers.

I wasn't afraid or depressed. I'd already found peace and was thinking about getting on with the next chapter of my life. That is *truly* what I was thinking about while getting ready that morning, being driven to the courthouse, and walking into court.

I can't remember whom I hugged, as it was all a blur, with so many people there in the hallway that I knew. One was my longtime personal/

business lawyer, Keith Solar (also the adopted papa of our doggie, Rocky). Keith had been with me since I started my company back in 1997, and he was like an older brother to me. We were extremely close, and Stevo loved him too. Also, some friends of mine from Michigan were there, including my best girlfriend, "J."

I was *not* surprised by my sentence, but I *was* shocked, however, that the judge apparently hadn't really read the case and didn't fully appreciate the extent of my cooperation. I had the feeling that his mind was already made up.

My attorneys had been told by the clerk that Judge Burns was going to have me remanded that morning. There was not going to be any "60 days to put my house in order." My house was already in order.

I could tell that Burns had been looking forward to this day for a long time. There weren't going to be any surprises. If there was a proverbial book, he was going to be throwing it. Being in court is like participating in a kabuki theater show. Everyone knows their roles and their lines, and everyone stays in character.

My attorney made a few simple corrections to the probation report, which said that I was 5'4" when in fact I'm 5'5". And frankly, who cares, but everyone is being meticulous. I felt like a stick figure—"Everybody's talking at me, I don't hear a word they're saying, only echoes of my mind." The Court had thoughtfully provided an overflow room for the expected hordes, but in truth, no more than 60 people showed up, and a third were lawyers or media.

The statutory maximum for my three counts was 15 years, so that was the starting pitch count. The only suspense left in my mind was to see if Burns was going to find some way to give me life without parole or go all in for the death sentence.

Although my attorney was no Daniel Webster, he made his case: I'd been enormously helpful, and I still had good works that I could do in the community. I'd gone astray (at least he didn't use the lamb thing there), and he argued that a "downward departure" was warranted. *Downward departure* is a legal term equivalent to begging for mercy.

Look, Judge, you got 15 on the table to play with, so let's acknowledge all the good things Ms. Champion-Cain has done in her life and cut her some slack.

And then I was able to give my allocution statement. That's where I apologized, and I meant every word.

Then the U.S. Attorney's Office got their turn. Here's a portion of the statement from Aaron Arnzen, Chief Major Frauds and Public Corruption Section, U.S. Attorney's Office, San Diego, CA:

> "And she created, forged and phony documents year after year, time after time, and when the heat was turned up or the spotlight was on, Ms. Champion-Cain turned on the forgery machine. She created fake e-mails. She had any number of layered manners of deception, and finally, Ms. Champion-Cain obstructed the federal investigation by changing, hiding and destroying evidence."

I had to admit that really stung, but it was all true.

Mr. Arnzen continued:

> "Your honor, for those reasons, the United States thinks that a 130-month sentence is appropriate."

Perhaps I'd caught a break. Now remember, Arnzen, we made a deal. I agreed to tell all, and you agreed to acknowledge my good work with a reduced sentence, which is exactly what you've done. With good behavior and some other "downward" adjustments, I could be out in eight or nine years, maybe less.

My attorney stepped up and said, "130 works for us, and we're good to go." I'm thinking justice is being served.

And then the judge got his turn.

The Court: "My understanding is that only two people have been charged criminally."

Here, he's referring to me and to Crispin Torres.

Mr. Arnzen: "That's correct, Your Honor."

The Court: "Is it anticipated that other defendants will be charged?"

Mr. Arnzen: "Yes, Your Honor."

More shoes are going to drop, and they aren't Manolo Blahniks. The government is going to want me around for testimony and further input, so I'm thinking the sun'll come out tomorrow.

And then Burns does a Crispin Torres on me.

Judge Larry Alan Burns had a reputation, richly deserved, and he wasn't going to disappoint. The two sides had made a deal, but Burns's position was that you can take your "understanding" and stuff it. What followed was 30 minutes of legal explanations and discourse that ended with something along the lines of: "I could have given you 40 years by my way of thinking, so consider yourself lucky that you only got 15, which is the max under the law, but if I had my way, trust me, it would have been more."

But then Burns gets into the weeds, and because I wasn't allowed to speak, I simply had to bite my tongue.

> **The Court:** "Restitution is important, but I'm just not sure that restitution is realistic at this point. There is nothing that has come up that convinces me that there's a lot of money out there to be recouped.
>
> "If you have ever been the victim of a fraud, you know the hopelessness that follows when you realize the money is gone. No prospect that you're going to get it back."

That perception by Burns was deeply frustrating. I knew that there was a lot of money coming back, and I knew from where. I knew where the bodies were buried, and for some reason, my attorney neglected to stand up and remind the Court that of the $170 million that the receiver considered to be "net losses," more than $80 million of that had already been paid back by Chicago Title. More than 100 investors had already received approximately 75 cents on the dollar. And there were more settlements coming, including the last three "big" cases, the institutional ones still being litigated.

***

I'm telling this story from my prison cell at the Federal Correctional Institution, Dublin, California. But it's for sure that there are more indictments coming. There is more criminal litigation coming. There are clawbacks coming. There are swords poised and more than a few people, certainly including Chicago Title, are going to be falling on them.

No excuses. And the wheel is going to keep spinning for a while.

***

I've begun to think that prison is a good thing—everyone should try it for a while. It's a good place to channel *Cool Hand Luke* and "get your mind right."

Sometimes very good people make very bad decisions in a variety of ways. We get blinded by a possible shortcut, and we believe we can fix it later before anyone finds out. Never again. I had multiple choices, but I chose badly and picked a dangerous path, one that could never end well. I was running hard and fast, and I wanted to please people. Maybe good intentions on a misguided path. I believe in atonement. I will come out of prison better and stronger and smarter.

A mentor of mine said that you learn more in life and in business from the bad decisions you make than you do from the good or lucky ones. I felt trapped, but I didn't look hard enough for good decisions. I was weak and took easier paths. I know now that there are always better options.

The truth is, I was desperate, and didn't want to be stopped. When the moment came, I gave in to my worst instincts. There were other paths to take; I just couldn't see them at the time.

I remain an optimist. I've never been depressed. I've experienced grief and sadness in my life, and the loss of loved ones, but I've never experienced depression. I'm not on suicide watch.

I'm going to be in prison for a while, but like the Terminator, I'll be back. Here is my allocution statement in full:

> *Your Honor,*
>
> *I have written down my thoughts, as I want to make sure I can articulate to you and to my victims the feelings about what I have done.*
>
> *First, I want you to know that I absolutely understand the gravity of my crimes and the horrible impact they have had on my victims and their families, as well as on my own family, friends, and community. I also am deeply sorry to have disappointed all the women entrepreneurs who looked up to me as an accomplished female executive and role model. I behaved in ways that were horrific, and I made terrible choices that did not align in any way with my own values system.*
>
> *My actions have hurt so many people . . . I feel terrible for my victims . . . all of them . . . even the ones I have never met. These are people who trusted me or trusted others involved with me. For over a year I have wanted to reach out to all of them, but upon the advice of my attorneys not to undermine the government's case against me and others, I did not do so. Yet my number one goal has been and will continue to be helping my victims recover as much as they can from my terrible crimes. I also stand ready to continue to assist the government in its efforts to recover ill-gotten gains from willing participants and benefactors.*

Why would a woman who was brought up in a loving environment with the gift of education, who has worked hard all her life, who has loved her family and friends fiercely . . . WHY? Why would I, who had such privileges and people who have mentored, supported and loved me through the years, why would I engage in such horrendous conduct? I have been evaluating my life and why I would ever do such terrible things, especially since really all I have ever believed in throughout my life is helping and pleasing people. Yet along the way, coming out of the recession of 2008, I reached a desperation point. I worked hard to generate wealth for my family, my friends and myself as we all struggled to make it out of that dark economic hole. I kept trying to pull deals together, to be creative in the re-creation of my business, but I kept failing. I panicked and felt I needed to support an image of who people believed "Gina Champion-Cain" was . . . but it wasn't real. The emperor had no clothes.

I deserve to be punished, and I promise that I will use the future to take what I have done and the impact it has made to really help others . . . this time, in the wholesome and charitable ways that I was taught by my Grandparents and Parents, and that I had always demonstrated prior to this segment of my life. I truly believe that there is a light out of darkness. I believe in the sun even when it's not shining. I have felt the darkness of dramatic changes with incomplete goodbyes and uncertain futures. But the light of God's love surrounds me and offers everyone hope. I am committed to be the light to help others less fortunate than I have been. I want to be the light in the darkness . . . through uncharted times and during urgent challenges. I will use my time while incarcerated to help teach others less fortunate than I in whatever ways I can, whether it be basic math, grammar and reading skills, or more advanced concepts related to real estate and business.

I will also teach others the fundamentals of successful entre-preneurship with the emphasis on using a moral compass to navigate through business' sometimes treacherous waters.

The wounds will eventually heal although they will leave scars forever. But those scars won't impede what I will do the rest of my life . . . and that is to help people overcome hardships, understanding professional right from wrong, and giving comfort in times of need. I can figure out how to help people the right way because, if nothing else, I have shown that I can be effective in whatever I put my mind to do. I know I can use my skill set for the betterment of others and I will seek forgiveness and do the right thing by giving back and never slipping down this dark hole again.

Thank you, Your Honor.

*** ***

CHAPTER 28

Redemption
and Atonement

Thank God we all get a second chance.

A s I sit in prison with time to reflect, I think about why the women in Dublin committed the crimes that put them here. The ladies I've met so far on my short journey have many varying reasons. Mostly, these reasons involve the unfortunate reality of the grips of addiction, often the result of trying to alleviate the pain of abuse or trauma. Other reasons involve their relationships with very bad influencers, again mostly the result of enduring years of abuse, compounded by a lack of self-esteem. Add to that the pressures of family, children, parents, and the ever-present issue of money, and you can begin to see how the system works to destroy people.

And that leads me to telling you more about my *why*.

I'm not sure I'll ever be able to answer that question adequately, but what I've come up with so far, in part, revolves around an "I'll show you" thought process. Being here in prison, away from the "noise" of everyday life, has given me the ability to look inward in a realistic manner. In keeping with my desire to "show you," I think about the aggregators, the bundlers, and the majority of the investors. Wealthy White Men. The same men I'd been up against my entire career.

But I didn't want to hurt anyone. I'd spent the entire seven years of the scam crafting a very detailed and achievable exit strategy whereby I could reimburse everyone. The act of my defiance was considered, in my mind, to be only a short-term loan, a way to raise money to build businesses. I employed almost 800 people, and everyone got health insurance. I was deeply active in the community and in several charities.

My intent was to just get the ball rolling, and then take the operation over with legitimacy, the same as it began. However, it became a runaway train, with the greed of others simply growing exponentially, like an uncontrollable virus. And, frankly, the "high" of being able to do so many good things for others became *my* addiction. I knew that I was giving away money that wasn't mine, but maybe in an arrogant way, I thought I could use it better than the investors.

But I know the insanity. I know the crime, and I know that what I did was wrong. There is no attempt for justification. What I did was *wrong*, and I am deeply remorseful and sorry because I hurt many, many people, and it has never been in my character to do so—I've always been the opposite. Yet for some reason, in my late 40s, I took a terrible turn, out of weakness, where I gave up on my religion and my upbringing, and in a moment of deep personal frustration, simply decided to say, "I'm going to do things I want to do for others using the money of people who would otherwise never agree to part with it for the reasons I aspired to."

I feel good in prison, I deserve to be here and to be held accountable for my actions. And my acceptance of this is what has allowed me to integrate into the prison program so quickly. I'm working for the education department here, helping the assistant warden, and also teaching classes to other inmates. In some way, this is a part of my destiny, part of my journey, and I'm determined to achieve excellence while I'm here. My story is still being written, and I think the next chapters of my life will be called "Redemption and Atonement."

*** ***

CHAPTER 29

The Receiver, Restitution, and More Indictments

The wheel is always spinning.

As of today, in the spring of 2022, there are several developments. A mandatory settlement agreement was noticed by Judge Allison Goddard, and everybody—absolutely everyone—lawyers et al., was required to attend. It happened in January, but nothing was resolved. The trial date had been set for December 2022, but even money says there will be no trial. In addition, Ovation Finance made a settlement with Chicago Title over the past few weeks, which is on the order of $45 million. They may have actually gotten back more than they invested or lost. Accounting is a magical skill.

Benjamin Galdston got a certified settlement with Chicago. Kind of a double-double maneuver. He got a class financial settlement for his original 47 investors and then picked up another 20 to 30 who defected from ABC Funding, Joe Cohen, and Kim Peterson. You can't argue with a "take the money and run" investor.

In addition, unrelated to the various settlements, there are at least two criminal indictments under consideration, but they haven't been filed yet. As indictments and settlements evolve, it becomes more possible that my sentence will be substantially reduced. One can only hope.

*** ***

CHAPTER 30

"First, Let's Kill All the Lawyers."

—Shakespeare

From Neil Senturia

In the course of writing this book, I ended up becoming friendly with only one attorney. There were more than nine different lawsuits with multiple legal eagles at the time of this writing, but there was only one class-action lawyer, and his name is Benjamin Galdston. He is a measured fellow, and he helped me navigate the nuances of the legal battlefield. As the kid at the ballpark says, "Ya can't tell the players without a scorecard."

How did we meet?

Gina was serviced by more than a dozen "bundlers," and I tried to track each of them down to talk about their view of the scheme. A few would talk to me on the record, some off the record, some with remorse, some with anger. It ran the gamut. Unfortunately, the major player, Kim Peterson, would not talk, as he is still one of the key figures in the litigation.

But one guy I called did answer the phone: Tom Dobron.

I started politely, but in short order, Mr. Dobron hung up the phone.

And then 12 minutes later, my phone rang, and it was Benjamin Gald-ston. He indicated that I was not to call his client ever again. Point taken. But then after I'd agreed to his terms, we kept talking. I told him that I was writing a book, and I shared some of what I thought I knew; and without compromising any legal ethics, he listened, and in the end agreed to speak to me from time to time.

Over the next six months, we spoke a few times, always in the service of my trying to understand what was filed, what it meant, and in particular, the legal strategy being employed.

But class-action litigation carries some significant risks, the primary one being that you do all the work, and you could end up with nothing. Most lawyers like to be paid hourly for their work, regardless of the outcome. In a class-action suit, you may get 25 to 35 percent of the winnings—but only if there are any. In this case, the only deep pocket was Chicago Title, and it wasn't clear at the beginning that they were culpable. Most fingers were pointing at Gina and her company, ANI, which would prove to be nothing more than a house of cards with very few tangible assets, and certainly not enough to make up the $175 million shortfall.

A class-action lawyer is usually disliked by the white shoes who get paid hourly, because if he prevails, he sets the bar, he sets the deal, he sets the settlement number and the other attorneys, and their clients are left with Hobson's choice, often paraphrased as "Take it or leave it."

Galdston is an outsider and a bit of a gambler, which is why I gravi-tated to him. His words:

> *Everything has to start with the genesis. It is May 2019 and*
> *I get approached by a friend who lives in Mission Hills—he's*
> *a neighbor of Gina's, 20-year friendship with this guy, and*

he says to me, "Hey, I have an opportunity to invest in a deal, and it just doesn't smell right."

And I agree to do a little digging. He tells me the whole premise, and I say, "You know, there's something wrong here. It doesn't pencil out. And the rate of return just smells too good."

My entire career has been focused on what we call Open Market Securities Fraud, publicly traded stocks, multimillion, multibillion-dollar cases. I'm not really focused on small Ponzi schemes, local stuff. Usually at the end of those, you're picking over the bones of a dead carcass. The money has been spent; there's really nothing to be had.

So the first thing I did was look at whether, in the hard-money lending world, financing liquor licenses was a real thing. Are there other lenders? There are always competitors, nobody corners a big market, and I wanted to see if anybody else was doing this. When I was growing up, I worked in bars, nightclubs, in the Bay area. I saw that these businesses had tight margins and were always looking for money. And I knew the value of that liquor license. I was a kid, but guys talk.

The deal didn't strike me as bizarre, but it struck me as unusual, and I thought that if there is one person making these loans, surely there must be others. Because, you know, an opportunity loves competition.

I went looking. I called a friend of mine in the Central Valley who's pretty savvy in real estate hard-money lending, and I talked to him about it, and he goes, "Never heard of it."

Made no sense. How could one person have, sort of, discovered this golden opportunity and have millions and millions of dollars of loans and a portfolio, and nobody else is marketing to that demand? First red flag: nobody else is doing this kind of deal.

And then you gotta figure that if this is really a big business, a $400 million business, why are the applicants going to Joey Bag-o-Donuts who owns a small restaurant in Mission Hills? Where are the institutions or private equity?

And then the mother of all red flags: my friend says, "You have to be invited. Invitation only. Don't ask too many questions."

And I tell him to run away as fast as he can. And that's it. Nothing more until July 2019, when I notice that the SEC has filed a securities fraud complaint. It alleges that the violation had been going on for seven years and that almost a half billion dollars was involved. And the only people they're naming are Gina Champion-Cain and ANI. Huh. They seem to go to extraordinary lengths to not name Chicago Title in the complaint. And that gets my attention. They don't name the essential party in the process.

Chicago is owned by Fidelity National Title. Last time I looked, they had a market cap of $11 billion, Fortune 500. Not chump change.

So how does something like this happen? It happens because it has the veneer of legitimacy and success. This is what Bernie Madoff was so good at—he was the former head of NASDAQ. How could you doubt that? What possible reason would he have to be a criminal?

This program operated for as long and as big as it did for one reason and one reason only: Chicago Title. If you look at the marketing materials, if you look at Gina's communications with investors, that is the linchpin. That is the one thing that she points to over and over and over again. "Your money is absolutely safe. Why? Because it's not in my pockets, it's in escrow."

Okay, two possibilities. Number one, if you think your government is doing its job, you would assume that they'd done a very thorough investigation and run every lead to the ground before they even filed their complaint, and that they'd concluded, beyond a shadow of a doubt, that Chicago Title wasn't involved, not culpable. That's door number one.

But maybe it's Monty Hall: "Okay, let's see door number two."

Maybe Chicago Title has bullied the SEC and the DOJ into believing that they had nothing to do with this, that they were duped too, and that they were the victim. And the fact that Chicago was nowhere to be seen in the complaint, that got my real interest.

Now, you know from reading this book so far that on August 28, 2019, Gina went to Los Angeles to meet with the SEC, and one day after that meeting, she pled guilty and a receiver was quickly appointed. And with that appointment, there was a "bar" order that laid out the specific claims that were reserved for the receiver. And normally you'd make these claims as broad as possible. You want to close everyone else out and shut the door to other litigation. A bar order should tell the world that no one can file any litigation until the receiver decides the next steps. But Allen Matkins, the law firm representing receiver Krista Freitag, didn't do that.

More from Galdston:

All the bar order says is that you can't sue the "ANI entities." It doesn't mention Gina, and it doesn't mention Chicago. WTF. There's no way this goes on for as long as it did without them knowing and somebody on the ground being involved.

My initial thought was, "Chicago Title's in on this. There's no way they're not in on this." How high it goes up, I don't know."

At this point, Galdston has the "Maybe this is bigger than I thought" idea, and he begins to think like a class-action lawyer.

More from Galdston:

I realize that I can sue Gina, Chicago, Cris Torres, Rachel Bond, the whole gang. The Receiver lawyers left the door wide open, and I file the first retail investor complaint. The Allred complaint. November 4, 2019.

In the class-action game, like many things, it's good to be first.

Galdston puts out a press release.

Phone off the hook. And it's a lot of the smaller investors. And one of the reasons they join is that they don't have to be public, they don't have to look like idiots to their friends. They're embarrassed, and they want to hide their shame.

And they don't want to hire their own lawyer, the kind they have to pay by the hour. If your loss is 50 or a hundred grand, you can't afford to go it alone.

My expectation is that there's going to be a tidal wave of litigation, and unlike many Ponzi schemes, this one has a deep-pocket participant in Chicago Title. Blood in the water.

So I call up Chicago in the middle of December 2019, and ask for a settlement meeting. Their response is to suggest I die and pound sand. We will see later how much sand is left on their beach.

In my view, this was a mistake. A rational defendant would settle early because that sets up a gambler's choice. The investor can take a known deal, or he can roll the dice in litigation.

And the most troubling thing about dice is timing. Time value of money versus aggravation versus dropping dead (some of the investors are in their late 80s) before you get your hands on the dough.

The reason a defendant might learn to like me, the class-action lawyer, is because they only have to deal with one rapacious lawyer instead of 20.

Now consider the Chicago attorneys. Their game is delay, delay. Good for legal fees, and while Chicago might eventually owe 150 million at some point in the future, while they haggle now, they're making 15 to 20 percent per year in the stock market over the past two years. And they're playing with house money. Chicago has insurance. My goal is to get into court if I can't settle.

And the receiver—well that is a whole 'nother animal—they get paid well feasting on the remaining assets, so while they're recovering some of the money, they're also getting paid by that money. Could be a zero-sum gain where the investors get very little.

And then the Black Swan event, March 2020—COVID. And you can't get into court. Dead in the water for almost a year.

Look, let me go off the reservation for a minute. If you're Steve Strauss (attorney for Chicago Title), on day one you tell Chicago that you're going to lose, but it will take three years to get into court (the trial date is set for December 10, 2022), and then you tell your client that we will appeal, and that takes another two years—so when the dust settles, and after you collect your insurance money, the whole loss to Chicago is no more than a rounding error on 11 billion, but the investor, the little guy, he's trapped in a system that is simply beyond his understanding. You know, justice delayed is justice denied.

Litigation, depositions, and hearings took up most of the year, but at the very end, in a clever maneuver, and with a deep understanding of timing, in December 2021, Mr. Galdston settled his lawsuit with Chicago Title on behalf of his original 47 clients. But it was not a class-action settlement; it was a "certified financial settlement." There was no way Galdston could get his class certified (legal issues), but he got the next best thing—a "certified financial settlement" for his 47 original clients. And then he got something else, which he admits he never thought he'd ever have a chance to get. He got the right for a few weeks to announce to any other investors who wanted to that they could join his settlement.

That meant that other investors who may have been standing on the sidelines could now join the settlement, knowing with certainty the financial nature of the outcome. In other words, you get to know the actual dollar number you're going to receive before you sign your name. A no-obligation free look.

A few weeks later, Galdston and I spoke again.

The number of people who'd joined in (you remember about rolling the dice) had ballooned from his original 47 to just under 100. He'd boxed out the receiver and had outmaneuvered several of the other fancier law firms. Their leverage was now dramatically diminished, with fewer investors left unrepresented and not settled.

He'd made individual fee agreements with each investor for a percentage. He would not tell me the exact numbers, but let's ballpark his fee at 25 percent, and let's ballpark the recovery from Chicago Title at around 73 cents. And the total amount at issue, he wouldn't tell me, but let's ballpark that at $9 million.

In the end, the details aren't critical. What Galdston had done was get a settlement from a company that didn't want to make one. And on his way out the door, he sent one more "Fuck you" to the receiver and the remaining white-shoe law firms, but that's a tale for him to tell another time.

What I found fascinating was that Galdston was motivated, of course, by making money, but he was also motivated by what my shrink and I call "redemption and revenge." He wasn't anointed with the white-shoe Ivy league imprimatur of many of the other lawyers, all feeding at the trough. He had something he wanted to prove. It's what pushed him his entire life. He'd become a lawyer later in life and had something to prove. And then he magically pulled off not just the settlement, but one more trick—one that I've agreed to not disclose. The litigation and the twists and spins will go on for a long time. For now, all good books have to come to an end.

But Benjamin Galdston's desire to win came from the same feelings that guys like Tom Brady had. Galdston was fueled by being "dismissed." He didn't own any "white shoes," and he was relegated to the sidelines in the minds of some of the other lawyers from the more prestigious firms.

So . . . I leave you with this: Do you think that maybe Gina had something to prove? Maybe to herself, maybe to her father? The impostor syndrome is as virulent as the COVID-19 pandemic, and its effect and power will far outlast any virus. It is embedded deep in the souls and psyches of competitive people.

Many of us are driven by the need to finish up old business or the desire to redeem ourselves from our pasts, and fueled with deep-seated fury and rage, we're determined to "show them" once and for all that we belong on that stage.

And most of us make the effort legally.

But then again . . . some don't.

*** ***

CHAPTER 31
Letters from Prison

Dublin Satellite Prison Camp

5675 8th Street – Camp Parks

Dublin, CA 94568

Cell 263 – Inmate #96841298

On March 31, 2021, Gina was led out of the courtroom in handcuffs. She spent the next 43 days being bounced between various jails, prisons, and holding facilities, including three weeks of quarantine because of COVID, on her way to a more permanent arrangement.

During that time, nobody told her anything, and she endured various indignities—including lack of food, clothing, and communication—visited upon her with furious anger and the tyranny of evil men (with apologies to *Pulp Fiction*). But in the end, she survived and finally ended up at the Dublin Federal Correction Facility (FCI) to join the other 110 women serving time there.

What I (Neil) saw in Gina during the time we spent together was an absolutely unimpeachable sense of optimism. She truly believed that she could take the ANI empire public and that she could pay everybody back. And she believed that she could stop the madness of this Ponzi scheme and return to society with clean hands.

Her detractors would argue that those are the fantasies of a delusional sociopath. Her supporters would argue that she had incredible charisma and fortitude, that nothing was out of her reach, and that she would be capable of the magic tricks necessary to undo the sins of her past. After all, stranger things . . .

After Gina got settled at Dublin, she began to write letters to Barbara and me. And the first ones sounded like she'd landed at a summer camp.

She wrote: "FCI is called Club Dub . . . there are no cells, and they have wooden doors with windows in every room that you can open for fresh air. The grounds are beautiful with lots of trees, and a large rose garden that the inmates tend to. They have a huge workout facility at FCI, a movie room where they hold weekly movie nights with popcorn and cotton candy, as well as dining halls that are both outside and inside. It is the nicest female prison in the country."

On her fifth day at Dublin:

"The women here have bonded and formed a tight community—caring and passionate beyond belief. Completely different than the outside world. There isn't jealousy, ego, or competitiveness. My incarceration will not last forever, and I am planning for the best accomplishments. The future is bright with hope."

Many of the letters talked about legal strategy with respect to Chicago Title and the numerous lawyers, hers included. Who did what to whom and why aren't they doing more indictments of the other crooks in the scheme?

It's clear that she didn't pull this off by herself. What is taking so long to find the other rats leaving the sinking ship?

Even though she's facing 15 years in prison, Gina is busy making plans for the future.

She wrote: "Whoever said that prison is boring certainly did not have my prison life. I have a job in the education department, and I am teaching a restaurant operations and management program in the prison so that when they get out, they will have options in the hospitality industry. I have also begun my Paralegal License program."

The question that lurks at the bottom of this enthusiasm is what prompted Gina to enter this criminal endeavor in the first place. It is the core question we ask when we're confronted with irrational behavior, whether our own or others.

Why did Bernie Madoff, why did Elizabeth Holmes, why did the school shooters, why did the insurrectionists, why not the vaccine—the *whys* of life are what fascinate all of us. And especially when we do it ourselves. Easy to see in others and blind to our own eyes.

And so we come to the final question: *What is remorse?*

In February of 2022, several things occurred.

First, Gina had a seven-hour deposition under the scrutiny of a lawyer for Chicago Title. It was a relentless grilling. He asked her the question that is posed to most people who end up in prison:

Chicago lawyer: "Why did you do it, when you seemingly had everything?"

Gina tried, but couldn't really answer him. She mumbled stuff about wanting to help people and make other people rich.

Chicago lawyer: "But you weren't making other people rich; you were stealing to make yourself rich."

And it was at this moment that she finally and fully admitted her culpability and remorse. She didn't cry in front of the lawyer, as that's not her nature, but when she went back to her bunk, she broke down.

Gina: "I can't believe I did this to my beautiful life and to my beautiful husband and to my friends, family, and community. I will never forgive myself. What a waste of a life. I really screwed up our [she was always thinking about her husband, Steve] beautiful life."

The day after that deposition, an article written about her, by Chris Pomorski, ran in *Bloomberg Businessweek*. It was not flattering, to say the least. It painted her in very dark hues. And, of course, lots of people read it. Pomorski had contacted many of her former employees and so-called friends. They were not kind. Perhaps revisionist history.

Gina's parents read the article and were devastated. Gina said:, "But I am not this horrible person. The article makes me out to be a complete failure, almost makes me never want to get out of this prison."

This is the moment when many incarcerated individuals say: *I am not what I was, I can change, and I will not give up.*

Gina wrote a letter to me the next day, saying, "Yesterday I felt like the lowest scum of the earth, but the next morning, sitting on my bunk, I saw the sunrise, and I knew I was stronger and better than how I was depicted, and I can change, and when I get out I can be a force for good and positive change."

The story is not complete yet. There are more depositions and more litigation between the various financial elephants. And then there is the Rule 35B hearing in March or April of 2022, which might shorten Gina's sentence.

Like all lives, there is complexity. None of us is one color. All of us are prisms that reflect and refract. No apologies. She did the crime. She will do the time.

I've spent several years teaching entrepreneurship at Donovan State Prison in San Diego. I've interacted with more than 150 of my favorite felons, from short-timers to lifers. What I can tell you is that no one wants to be known only for the worst thing they did in life.

*** ***

Notes from
the Authors

Neil Senturia
Before Glengarry Glen Ross

It was 1972, I was living in Los Angeles—having graduated from the American Film Institute—and I was laboring in the field known as screenwriting, which bears a close resemblance to being unemployed. And like just about everyone in Hollywood, I needed to find some kind of job that I could work at to pay the rent while still having time left to focus on my writing, the dream that had brought me to La-La Land.

I found an ad in the *Los Angeles Times* for a telephone sales position. I went to an office on Robertson Boulevard, and the sales manager informed me that the position was a seated one, with no connection to yoga poses. Rather, it was a simple "You sit down here in this cubicle, read from this script, make 120 calls during your shift, and try to get some dumb sonofabitch to buy the crap we're selling. You get two weeks, and if you don't make four sales, you're fired." To this day

I remain of the opinion that this gentleman was the model for Alec Baldwin in *Glengarry Glen Ross*.

It turned out that I was really good at this telephone game. In fact, after 30 days, I was actually the best in the company. What did we sell? We called banks across the country, using what was known as the "Blue Book." We would masquerade as their usual "Xerox toner" provider, and with three or four innocent questions and some clever manipulation of numbers, we could figure out what machine they had and then explain that we'd be shipping them "their usual order," and of course, "Betty, we'll mark it to your attention." This toner boiler room was no different from the one run by the Wolf of Wall Street—just a different product.

Of course, I couldn't use my own name. It wasn't just that I might get into trouble and would need plausible deniability, but rather, my major concern was that someone might recognize my name at the Oscars, winning for best original screenplay! I was a writer, so I invented a character, someone with charm and wit and a trace of a Southern accent. I picked the nom de plume of Paul Biegler, the attorney in the movie *Anatomy of a Murder*. Since I'd gone to film school, this seemed like a good choice. After all, who wouldn't want to be Jimmy Stewart? And then I added the appellation of Colonel, as I'd been in the army as a Spec-4, and why shouldn't I take the promotion I so richly deserved? So when I called Betty, I announced myself as Colonel Paul Biegler, U.S. Army, Retired.

Let's be clear—Betty was the receptionist or secretary who answered the phone, and she didn't know anything about toner or a copying machine, other than how to put a piece of paper into it and call the repairperson if it broke. I was an actor making a living in a set piece that was a scam, and she was my unwitting co-conspirator.

I got up at 5:00 a.m. each day, went to the office, and starting at 5:30, I'd call the East Coast banks and companies and then work my way across the country with the time zones, ending up on the West Coast around 10:00 a.m. And then I'd go home and sit at my typewriter (that is *not* a misprint, it was a Smith Corona), and wage war in the trenches.

We were selling toner cartridges for $80 each, and the standard package always had six in them, so the order total was $480. We'd somehow determined that if an invoice was under $500, it would be paid without question, but above that, it would get scrutiny—and we did not want scrutiny.

And then to make sure the order would "stick," we'd call Betty the next day to "confirm and verify" the order and, of course, at the beginning we'd mention that we were recording the call for internal blah blah (and to have some kind of vague proof, if and when the head of purchasing would call and demand a refund)—and let me tell you that the phrase "We are recording this call" was said as quickly and as routinely as possible. *Just the facts, ma'am. Confirm the quantity, the address, and put the stuff in the mail.*

This toner racket was highly profitable. Our cost of goods was about $11 per cartridge. And the stuff we were shipping was not "Xerox" brand toner. But during the phone call, inadvertently, of course, we may have allowed Betty to think that she was getting the licensed brand rather than the toner we were sending, which was made by a fly-by-night organization in Texas, whose cost of goods was closer to $2, so you can see there was plenty of margin in this game. That black powder was masquerading as black gold.

But justification is a nuanced emotion, and I didn't have the time to take my thoughts on honor and deception to the Supreme Court. I needed to pay the rent while I pursued the goal of becoming Steven Spielberg. But did I know that we were involved in a "shady" and potentially illegal scheme? Yes. Did I continue to sell toner each morning? Yes.

After six months, I had an entrepreneurial epiphany of my own. If the owner of the company, cleverly called Standard Toner, was making a profit, and if I were the top salesperson, well, either pay me more or perhaps I should go into business and do it for myself. I shared my thinking with the owner, and to my great surprise, his thoughts on the topic of paying me more were the equivalent of drop-dead-die-and-pound-sand-and-go-fuck-yourself.

So the decision was made for me. There was one other guy in the office who was young, brash, and really good at the cold-calling game, and I suggested that we go off on our own together. He agreed. The next step was to figure out suppliers and phones and shipping. We'd learned the business on someone else's dime, and it wasn't that complicated. Within three months, we'd rented a warehouse, had 15 plywood cubicles covered in carpet to muffle the sound, 25 phone lines courtesy of AT&T, and we were up and running with our own business. And, of course, there was the delicious denouement that all entrepreneurs crave, the moment when I got to stick my head into Lucky's office (yes, that was the name of the owner), on my way out the door at the end of my last shift and tell him that he should listen carefully behind him, because the footsteps he would be hearing were my partner and me coming to bury him.

We stole some of the previous salespeople, we paid better commissions, and we made a better deal with the suppliers. We'd now entered and embraced the world of American capitalism, just two guys trying to make a buck.

And along the way, we printed money. A lot of money.

My usual routine: Wake up at 6:00 a.m., run the business in the morning, and in the afternoon pitch a TV pilot to CBS. I was living the dream. On Friday evenings, my partner and I would sit in the dumpy back office, have a scotch, take out the checkbook, pay ourselves, shake hands, and go home.

But let's return to that concept of shipping the goods. We had to send the toner packages to the customers, and to do that we had to use one of two ground-delivery services—in particular, UPS or the United States Postal Service (USPS). The mailmen were less expensive.

After about two years, we'd grown to be the second-largest telephone sales shop on the West Coast, and then one day I get a letter on the official letterhead of a "federal agency." I don't actually remember the exact organization, but the word *federal* was there, and it suggested that they wanted to come visit our offices and have a talk with us. It wasn't exactly a subpoena, but it was close enough for government work.

It had certain words in it referring to the USPS and mail fraud and felony . . . and the rest of the letter was a blur. It seems that shipping this toner through the mail was being viewed as something illegal.

I did a quick review of some books in the law library, which in relatively simple language indicated that mail fraud was a felony carrying a penalty of between 5 and 20 years. I called my partner and explained that I had a promising career ahead of me in Hollywood, and I did not want to live out the rest of my days in Mexico on the lam, or in a more local establishment with Bubba as my cellmate.

We responded politely to the letter and said we would be delighted to meet later the following week. And then in a scene right out of *The Sting*, we dismantled the entire warehouse, ripped out all the cubicles and phones, and the entire operation disappeared in five days. A junior "Fed" came to see us the following week. We begged, bartered, and apologized, using the classic defense of "Gee, Officer Krupke." And eventually the matter was dismissed with a very firm slap on the hand. The "evidence" was gone, we were gone, and frankly, they had bigger fish to fry.

And so, up close and personal, I had stood on the abyss and peeked over the edge. My partner and I were terrified, and for sure, I had no moral confusion: I was aware that we were running a scam. I'd dodged a bullet, and I knew it.

And that experience is why I chose to write about Gina Champion-Cain.

Barbara Bry
I have also been a woman in a man's world.

When I was a teenager, my parents got divorced, and my mother, Adelaide Bry, went to work at a large Philadelphia ad agency where she was paid less than the comparable men, and there was nothing she could do about it. She wanted to buy a house that she could easily afford, but still had to get a male friend to cosign on the mortgage.

I watched my mom reinvent herself, return to school, earn a master's degree in psychology, and become a best-selling author of self-help books. My mother helped me believe that I could succeed in the male-dominated world of business, and I earned an MBA from Harvard in 1976, at a time when few women were earning an MBA anywhere.

Like Gina, in the early part of my career, I was either the only woman in the room or one of only a few females. I experienced sexual harassment, and at various times was paid less than men who were doing the same job. As a result, I've started organizations and initiatives that empower women by bringing them together to support each other.

I knew Gina socially, and Neil and I ate at her restaurants. I admired her success in the male-dominated world of real estate development and her service on nonprofit boards. We were never asked to invest in the liquor-license loan program, and we didn't even know about it until it was shut down.

I remember my shock when I read the first newspaper article about the $400 million Ponzi scheme that she'd masterminded. I asked myself why she'd done this. What could have been going through her mind? How could she possibly have thought it would end in a good way? Didn't she understand that it was both illegal and wrong? As Neil and I talked with Gina, we learned more about her life—her fierce yearning to succeed in a male-dominated world, her desire to take care of others, and her aspiration to be viewed as ultra-successful.

I believe that Gina is truly remorseful for making bad choices and causing pain to so many people. I know that she wants to use the next chapter of her life, particularly her time in prison, to help others.

*** ***

Epilogue—Perceptions of Gina

We spent many, many hours talking with Gina before she was sentenced, and we continue to talk and correspond with her by email. In addition, we've interviewed a number of people who knew her through the many diverse times of her life.

Gina appears different to everyone, depending on how you've come to know her. She's a quartz prism that refracts light and reflects your perception of her reality. Snell's Law describes the relation between the angle of incidence and the angle of refraction, and it neatly describes what happens when the intersection of your world and hers occurs, often leading to complexity and confusion. In other words, how did this train wreck actually happen, and who was the conductor?

To that end, we will share some perceptions from a variety of individuals who were willing to speak with us. Note that many of the players were not at liberty to chat with us, since in fact their personal liberty was under discussion and review with various governmental agencies.

But here is a poor man's explanation of Snell's Law as it pertains to Ms. Champion-Cain.

The comments below are reconstructed from conversations and notes.

1. **"A": A woman who did some design work for the early restaurants.**

"I've known Gina a long time, and I did some design work for her in the beginning. I feel like I set her up. I felt close to her, but in the end I'm not sure anyone can get really close to her. I know a lot."

(Although we told each person that we were writing a book, this particular individual didn't want to share any other thoughts without being paid. For the record, we did not do that.)

2. **"B": A class-action attorney representing a group of investors. In addition, he represents one of the individuals who has received a subpoena and who was also a significant investor in the program, as well as bringing in other investors.**

This stuff is right out of the movies, where you might throw the other guy under the bus to save yourself. For sure, either way, this case has proven to be a full employment act for the litigation community. As of this writing, six different lawsuits have settled, but his has not.

He shared with us some thoughts about Della DuCharme, which we found valuable and have used in the book. For Della to participate in the fraud, it was not the small amount of money that Gina paid her, but rather it was the sense of belonging, of being part of a club that would never, under normal circumstances, have taken her as a member. Gina allowed Della, and to a lesser extent, Betty Elixman, to taste the "good life," and that is a powerful draw.

He summed it up in one sentence: "Gina made her feel important."

3. **"C": An investor. Approximate amount: $150,000.**

We had coffee in Little Italy, a neighborhood in downtown San Diego. He comes from a semi-famous family, and he was quite candid with us. He got involved because his sons got involved. And, of course, his sons got involved because they knew someone. It is classic stuff.

His children never solicited any other investors. "C" himself was always skeptical of the whole program but went along for the ride. If he lost the money, he wouldn't miss a meal. When the thing blew up, he joined a group of about ten other investors who got a good attorney and made a deal with Chicago and settled for 65 cents on the dollar.

What we found fascinating is that he says he did significant due diligence. He's not the kind of guy to blow a couple hundred grand without looking hard at the numbers, and in the end, he couldn't find the flaw and went in on the deal. This guy is no novice. He's run companies, has litigated against tough guys, and has done some sharp-elbow New York City real estate deals. But the prism would not reveal itself.

In the end, he asked himself a rhetorical question: "Was she smart enough, or were we stupid enough?"

So, one of the things about the prism that is Gina is that it was nearly impossible to find the truth. People looked at her, and the light kept bending until they ended up looking at themselves.

4. "D": An investor who agreed to speak to us. She invested approximately $100,000.

Her story is the same as most. Her husband was a friend of one of the children of one of the early investors. She and her husband are young, with two small children, and unlike some of the other investors, this loss is significant to them. They put too much of their net worth into the program.

She and her husband were in the deal for four years, and they *did* get some cash returned, ostensibly interest on their investment. But each time a note matured, she was asked if she wanted to take her money out or roll it over. Most of the time, she rolled. She got a 1099 form for her interest, and then of course, she paid taxes on that "interest."

It was all so simple—you think you're playing with house money until you don't have a house anymore. When she found out that the friend who introduced her got fees on her investment, she was angry. As the case ground on, her feelings became visceral, and she got physically sick from the financial loss, nearly 75 percent of her and her husband's net worth. Toward the end of our chat, she said, "I don't know what friendship looks like these days."

Prior to Gina's sentencing, the young lady was offered a chance to write a victim's statement. She did not; she told us she was simply emotionally exhausted and had to move on. But she's not a saint. She wants the wrongdoers to be punished. She wants them to feel "the gut wrench" that she has. She did have a slight smile at one point. She said that if she had put all that money into renovating her home, it would have been considered stupid and excessive. But as she said, "At least I would have a new kitchen and bathroom."

She knows that Chicago has the financial capacity, and she calls them "cowards" and feels they should do the right thing and pay the money back. She thanked us for listening to her story, but we can tell you that this interview really grabbed us around our throats. It put a deeply human face on the real cost of this fraud.

5. "B": The class-action lawyer. Déjà vu.

We had another chat.

The U.S. Attorney's Office filed a "5K" motion during the sentencing process. It described Gina's "substantial assistance," and it asked the sentencing court for a "downward departure" from the sentencing guidelines. As we know, Judge Burns did not think much of that motion. But Gina is going to get a second bite at the apple with what is called a Rule 35(b) motion, which is filed within the first year after sentencing. It asks the court to reduce a previously imposed sentence because of the defendant's "substantial assistance."

Some prosecutors do not consider simply providing information to be "substantial" unless it leads to something specific such as an "arrest, indictment or conviction."

And "B" told us that there are other shoes going to drop. He thinks that Della is a "target" at the grand jury. Grand juries are sealed, so we can neither confirm or deny, and neither can "B," but it makes for good gossip over a glass of wine. He believes that Betty Elixman is only a "subject."

You may remember the dialogue during Gina's sentencing between the USAO Attorney Aaron Arnzen and Judge Burns when the Court asked if "other defendants will be charged," and Arnzen answered, "Yes."

So this case and story are not over. And we can't yet know what we're not allowed to know. "B" told us that he's still in negotiations with Chicago. And so everyone keeps dancing.

6. "E": A bundler.

Gina and this gentleman became friendly through a mutual introduction. "E" was very clear about the fact that no one knew the whole story. He kept using the phrase "a grand puzzle," and noted that no one could see all the connections.

In the tech world, a communication network's value is "proportional to the square of the number of connected users of the system." But it seems in this case that none of the users were ever connected, and that's what allowed the program to stay in place for such a long time.

"E" was anxious to be of assistance in our telling of the story, but in the end, he couldn't tell us much that we didn't already know.

"E" was one of the active users of the Petco box, and he met Della there one night too. It does seem that "perks" go a long way in influencing one's behavior. We guess the question for all of us is: What's your price?

"E" told us that he always liked to look people in the eye as a means of due diligence. But, of course, as Malcolm Gladwell pointed out in his book *Blink*, it's not a really good way; we get fooled all the time.

"E" thought of Gina as unpretentious and humble, exciting and compelling, with a terrific reputation. She was successful and was active in the community. There's nothing unique about those perceptions. Every bundler and investor have said almost the same thing. And he confirmed what just about everyone else has mentioned, "Without Chicago, she had nothing." As he thought about red flags, he kept coming back to not being able to talk to Della directly. The network of users remains disconnected.

At one point in the conversation, we used the name Betty Boop as a placeholder, and he interrupted us to say we couldn't do that. It turns out that "Betty Boop" was how Gina referred to Betty Elixman. Gina liked to use nicknames.

Finally, we asked him for his guess on her prison time. His number was seven. But he said he would be fine if it were more than 15.

7. "F": A restaurant employee.

This gentleman was managerial and helped keep Gina's restaurant operations up and running. He worked at The Patio until the receiver took everything over.

What struck us in our conversation was his fierce loyalty and integrity. Gina tended to inspire that in her employees. At the height, Gina and ANI had nearly 800 employees. We're convinced that none of them knew anything about licenses or liquor except maybe how to have a beer after work.

This fellow was in charge of financial reporting systems. Like many of the ANI folks that we talked to, they thought of their jobs as careers that they would stay at for a long time. And when the news hit, it was visceral, and many could not believe that it was true.

"F" explained that the restaurant business is a tough one; it's difficult to make money. But he felt that with Gina, there would always be enough financial resources available, and that would be necessary because he was quite clear: "The restaurants by and large did not make money."

A friend of ours, a true restaurateur, a famous guy who knew his way around a dozen kitchens, looked at the various restaurants when the receiver took them over and put them up for sale. He was impressed with the concepts and the style and all the bells and whistles, but when he looked at the books, he expressed that "she doesn't really know how to run a restaurant. The numbers made no sense, there was no way to make a profit, the costs were out of control."

But "F" was a believer that with enough time, he could have implemented the necessary systems on purchasing and costs, but the truth is, that was just not at the top of Gina's list. She was going too fast to slow down.

8. "G": A former SEC lawyer.

"G" helped a group negotiate and recover money from Chicago Title. Although he prepared a lawsuit, he never filed it. His was a unique perspective, in that he's seen all sides of these kinds of cases and has represented both sides at various times.

He gave us two reasons why his group settled. First, "litigation is unpredictable." And the second is the risk that the receiver might take over the whole case, in which case, the investors sometimes see less than a dime in recovery, given the costs that continue to run with a receivership.

So, in the end, this fine legal mind decided to "take the money and run." We spoke to one of the clients in the group, and he expressed it this way: "I was thrilled with the result."

"G" told us that it's not uncommon to miss all the red flags that only become visible after the fact. The Madoff fraud case was called out early by financial-fraud investigator Harry Markopolos, but the SEC did nothing for another eight years. Things are always obvious in the rearview mirror.

During his preparation for the negotiation with Chicago, "G" did his own autopsy and asked a simple question: "How the hell could it be that not one of these escrows ever 'closed' over the years?"

"G" had a charming and jaundiced view of the American jurisprudence system, which comes from years in the courtroom. "You settle because you have no fucking idea what the judge is going to do in the end."

He dislikes and distrusts all sides of the system. Our kind of guy.

9. "H": A bundler.

This gentleman was quite polite and courteous, and also curious as to who the publisher of the book was going to be. We could not impress him with a big name because at the time, there was no name. He liked the idea of "the biggest woman-run Ponzi scheme in American history." We appreciated his approval. It seemed like everyone wanted to go to Hollywood on this ride, even if they lost money, might get indicted, and might be clawed back, but the lure of "the movies" seemed irresistible.

He said that he'd "heard" that Gina had been telling people that she had a deal with Netflix. From her mouth to their ears, but news to us at that point.

"H" was impressed that we were involved in the Jewish community. Maybe that was just foreplay, but it was hard to get him on the record with anything substantive. "H" is in one of the lawsuits, and he was quite open about that.

But we asked him the one question that everyone has asked him, as well as all the other characters in the play: "Did you suspect?" "H" gave us a tangential answer by reminding us of all the various individuals and companies that had done due diligence, the teams that had gone to Chicago Title with what was supposed to be a fine-tooth comb, and there you have it.

"H" didn't confirm or deny. He said that in the end, "I don't think anyone knows for sure." But he did muse on the fact that Gina had been "San Diego Businesswoman of the Year" and was on the board at the University of San Diego.

As we've said throughout this book, the obligation for Gina to keep up appearances must have certainly played into the scheme. If the emperor has no clothes, then get thee to Nordstrom as fast as possible, and bring a credit card. We loved chatting with "H." He ended with a comment that was echoed frequently: "On a personal level, I am fascinated."

Yup, that's what Gina did. She fascinated people.

10. "I": A landlord.

"I" told us that his initial meeting was eye-opening, as in Gina was wearing a revealing shirtdress. "I" is a very straight arrow, and we think he was surprised, to say the least. In addition, he remarked that Gina seemed disappointed that he'd brought another executive with him—a woman.

The financial arrangement, the tenant improvements, and the construction were complicated, as is the case in most real estate deals, and of course, there were lawyers. Every real estate deal has lawyers, disputes, threatened litigation, and she said/he said, but in the end, everyone got paid what they were owed.

Gina never missed a rent payment, not once, during the six years. She paid religiously right up until the last month when the receiver took over the assets.

A previous individual we spoke with was highly doubtful of her restaurant skills, but there were many times, in this case, that she paid "percentage rent," which is rent over and above the base rent, based on the success of the restaurant.

"I" said, "You don't pay percentage rent out of the goodness of your heart." So the jury is still out as to her restaurant-management skills. Bottom line: running a restaurant is a tough business.

11. "J": A business partner.

This guy offered some insight as to how Gina would do a deal.

This guy had a coffee shop, a simple café in Gina's neighborhood. She walks in one day, has a cup, likes the coffee, begins holding meetings in the café, buys the coffee for one of her restaurants, and within three months offers to invest in the café.

They ran the café for a while, and then she wanted to go big: buy "the Ferrari of roasters, and get into selling bags of coffee beans. "J" was in over his head and wanted to sell his share, and Gina agreed to buy him out.

"J" explained how the deal went down. Gina gave him a glass of wine, put a yellow pad in front of him, and told him to write down his number, which he did—$125,000—and she said yes and paid him, no negotiation. It makes her sound like a high roller, but in fact, the money for that deal came from the same place where almost all of the money came from—someone else's money at Chicago Title.

And then "J" stayed on and worked at the roasting company, and he transitioned into working in some other areas of ANI. Very few people quit Gina. He ended by saying, "She has a remarkable knack to enroll people in her vision."

12. "K": An early investor.

"K" started as a friend of Gina's, became an investor, lost money, and *remained* a friend. That's what's so striking about Gina. There was this aura about her that brought everyone in under one big tent and gave them comfort and confidence.

Not only did "K" invest, but also some of her friends, and one of her sons became a mini bundler. One of her comments was that "I thought our group were the only ones bringing in investors." That sentence was repeated often by others. Gina's ability to compartmentalize and make each group feel they were the only ones and very special, was remarkable.

The size of the scam was approximately $400 million, give or take a few nickels, and it was only when the SEC filed the complaint in August 2019 that people looked around at each other, shocked to find out the scope of the program and who else was in the deal. There was that moment of "I didn't know you were in the deal too."

The place of sadness and anger for "K" was the guilt that one of her sons feels for having been so trusting and bringing in his friends. That sense of betrayal by Gina has been spoken of by others. It is the darkest part of her—that she never really understood the impact this scam would have on people, not just economically, but emotionally. It's the classic "How could I have been so stupid and not seen?"

"K" likened Gina to a "mad professor" ginning up another deal while the ink on the first one wasn't even dry. Others have used the phrase *whirling dervish*.

The twin dragons that haunt this deal for "K" are the loss of money and the loss of trust. Some handle it better than others, but in all of our interviews, the one consistent theme for almost everyone is feeling tricked, not only by Gina, but by Chicago Title.

But toward the end of the discussion, another theme emerged, and that was about money, about commissions. When "K" found out that people were being paid to bring investors into the program, she confronted Gina about why her son wasn't being paid as well.

The answer was unsatisfying, but what we admire is that notwithstanding all the friend-feeling stuff, in the end, she went to the mat for her children. That's what parents do.

We wonder if anything would have been different for Gina if she'd had children of her own.

13. "L": An attorney with parents who were investors through one of the funds: $200,000.

"L" is an attorney and knew several of the big institutional players in the program, and while he did not personally invest, his parents did. They had a wealth manager, one of the bundlers, and he was the one who convinced them to invest in the program. His parents weren't rich, and this was a significant number for them.

When "L" heard about the deal, it made no sense to him, but it's hard to confront your parents with your opinion. We are all someone's child, and sometimes family peace is best kept by biting your tongue.

"L" was one of a group of about 20 people who started a new bank in town. Gina wrote a check and went on the board of directors, but "L" only met her for the first time at the initial board meeting of the bank. As he said, "She talked a good game."

The subject of the liquor license and the bank business never intersected, and it wasn't until the day after the SEC filing in August 2019 that "L" found out about the scam, and of course, quickly became aware that his parents' money was at risk.

"L" did reinforce one consistent theme: Gina was not a very good businessperson. Her financial reputation among people who knew the facts was not a particularly astute one. He was not forgiving and said, "She was charming and she was pretty, and in my mind, she had criminal intent from day one."

"L" had a history of defending the little guy in a previous famous mortgage scam in San Diego, known as Pioneer Mortgage. In that case, there were lots of old Jewish folks in their 70s and 80s who got taken by a man named Gary Naiman.

What we admired about "L" was his fierce commitment to integrity and honor. At one point, he was contacted by his former law partner, Steve Strauss, who's now representing Chicago Title, and Strauss floated the question: "What do you think—do you have any interest in settling?" "L" told him, "My mom has cancer and died seven weeks ago." And sadly, his wife also died of cancer five years earlier. To top it all off, "L" was a small investor in one of the funds, Ovation, that put $25 million into the program, and is actively litigating with Chicago.

"L" was amazed, as almost everyone was, by the number of balls Gina could keep in the air at any one time. And he told one last story: There was a board meeting on a Monday, and Gina was in the conference room with everyone else, knowing that in two days, on that Wednesday, the SEC would accuse her of securities fraud, and the entire thing would blow up. And she never said a word. She didn't blink. Stone cold.

14. "M": New York investor, a "whale."

"M" is a big-time financier, a Wall Street bond trader. He's been an investor in multiple hedge funds, has worked as a bond trader for one of the big investment banks, and you could certainly say that he knew his way around major money.

He'd been friendly with Gina for a few years and visited her in San Diego. He'd gone to UC San Diego in the '80s and always felt that San Diego was home. He met Gina through a mutual friend with whom he played tennis. His "meet" with Gina seems to be the same story about 93 percent of the time. It was a good run while it lasted, and "M" was in long enough to get some of his money back, but he confessed, "I never took any interest out—foolishly. I had a big account on paper." And in the end, his losses were substantial in actual dollars.

But "M" was also a guy who saw the handwriting on the wall early, and he joined one of the larger groups trying to get some money back from Chicago. His group settled, so he has some sting to the whole thing, but he will never miss a meal. But he did have strong feelings about a clawback. No one should make a profit while others lose money.

He reiterated how effective Gina was in shielding Bill Adams, the "Wonder Boy" liquor-license lawyer; and Della DuCharme, in the escrow office at Chicago. "M" says that he did due diligence, but he could never get either of those folks on the phone. He reiterated that Gina had a reputation as a highly decorated entrepreneur, a Woman of the Year, and even had a "Day" named after her.

"M" said, "Gina just had this aura; it all seemed good. I never suspected. It was the ultimate con."

"M" was charming to a fault. He suggested that Donald Sutherland play Kim Peterson in the movie. For his own character, he liked Brad Pitt.

*** ***

Postscript

J ust before Gina was sentenced, the U.S. Marshals came into the courtroom from their magic side door, and afterward, they walked her out through that same door. She told us that she was then handcuffed, with shackles around her ankles, and experienced the usual strip search via the butt cheeks. They took away her dress, gave her an orange jumpsuit and a pair of sandals (three sizes too big and with two left feet), and she began to shuffle off until finally a female officer yelled at the Marshals, "Oh my God, get this poor girl some proper shoes that fit." And thus, her prison journey began.

It took a few minutes for us to realize that it was over, like waiting for a curtain call, perhaps. Finally, we walked out, and a friend of ours came up to us and showed us a website, @CTTHospitality.com. It was the website for Chicago Title, the very same Chicago Title that has been discussed throughout this book. And when we clicked on the icon that showed the various services they offer, and for which they have skills and expertise, the fourth item down listed under "Services" is a link labeled: LIQUOR LICENSE TRANSFER:

"When your liquor license needs to be transferred or sold, use Chicago Title escrow for the most efficient experience possible. Our knowledgeable team offers effective solutions that will keep your business running smoothly and successfully."

Yes, that is what it said, word for word. All we can say is this is a great country we live in. Where else can you advertise your effectiveness while at the same time paying out over $100 million for fraud and malfeasance. Only in America.

*** ***

Acknowledgments

I (Neil) am always amazed by the synchronicity of the world, and the unintended consequences of events and meetings that seem random, but we all know that life is definitely *not* random.

I've been writing a column on entrepreneurship for more than ten years for the *San Diego Union-Tribune*, and when she wasn't running for office or serving as an elected official, my wife, Barbara Bry, was co-writing the column. She had been a journalist for the *Los Angeles Times* and the *Sacramento Bee*.

One day in early 2020, I got an email from Gina Champion-Cain complimenting me on a particular column. I knew about her story and the plea, and Barbara and I knew her from social circles and the real estate business. So I called her—primarily to commiserate, and also to offer some kind words.

That led to a coffee in my office, which led to her wanting to tell her story, and finally her desire and willingness to share her entire journey. I did most of the interviews, Barbara read all of the transcripts and the many lawsuits, and then we wrote the book together. And yes, we're still happily married!

We're so blessed that many people have assisted us. In particular, I'd like to thank my longtime executive assistant, Nicole Rockstead, without whom I would be lost. Everyone thanks their assistant, of course, but in this case, we've been together for 29 years. She's been offered jobs by a dozen people who've come into my office and right in front of me have offered her more money than I'm paying her. But call it devotion or simply being hard of hearing, she's still with me—and it seems for the duration. I am very fortunate.

Even more to her credit, Gina became close to her, and I think that without Nicole, I might have been tossed to the curb more than a few times.

Then there's Helen Chang. She's a writer and editor and a guide to many authors. I helped her once when her business hit a bump, and she was appreciative, so when I turned to her for advice, her first suggestion was that I call the head of the Waterside publishing and literary agency, Bill Gladstone. We got along famously, and he instantly believed in the story. And although my heart has wavered from time, his never did. Authors often thank their publishers, but please allow me to do my thanking in capital letters: THANK YOU, BILL! His guidance was critical and appreciated, and it was also really astute. What more can you ask for from a publisher? He even tossed in two expensive lunches at a fancy beach restaurant.

Then we had the troops who did the heavy lifting. Karla Olson offered insights and advice. Helen Chang kept me focused. Our copy editor, Jill Kramer, made sure our sentences were logical and that the grammar was perfect. Kenneth Fraser designed an imaginative book cover that captures the essence of Gina; and our book designer, Joel Chamberlain, was intuitive and creative.

Then there are the pencil necks, the legal eagles, without which a Ponzi scheme cannot be unraveled. Most of them were either suing or defending and didn't take much interest in my inquiries. But one fellow, Benjamin Galdston, proved to be the exception. He never breached any ethics, but he was critical in educating me on the law and helping me understand who did what to whom and why it was brilliant or stupid. And all this while he himself was in the fray—and ultimately triumphed. A very clever attorney.

I am also deeply grateful to the many liquor-license loan victims and business associates of Gina who shared their stories and perceptions so that we could provide their point of view in this book. There's no revisionist history here. This was a major crime, the largest woman-run Ponzi scheme in American history.

As for our children, we have four between us. Barbara and I are a blended family, sort of like a martini with just a pinch of vermouth. We've been together for almost 30 years, and for this last acknowledgment, I need to be very clear: there would be no book without my wife, Barbara, and I think it's fair to say, at least from my point of view, that there would be no life for me without her either.

Like many stories, the last chapter is not yet written. More will come over time. The network of crookery is wide and wicked, and like any good one-reeler in the movie business, you have to come back next week to see if Pauline is rescued from the railroad tracks.

Stay safe and stay well, and all best wishes,

Neil and Barbara

About the Authors

Neil Senturia has lived by the rule that grand passion will take you further than good grades. He attended the American Film Institute, spent time in Hollywood writing sitcoms, then transitioned to real estate, developing more than two million square feet of new construction. He finally turned to technology, where he was the cofounder or CEO of nine start-ups over 25 years. His idol is psychologist/author Daniel Kahneman.

Barbara Bry, Neil's spouse, was a business writer for the *Sacramento Bee* and the *Los Angeles Times* before becoming a technology entrepreneur. She served on the San Diego City Council and is the founder of Athena San Diego, an organization focused on empowering women in the San Diego innovation economy. Her idol is her mom, Adelaide Bry, who broke many glass ceilings.

*** ***